What people are saying about …

Soul Shaping

"*Soul Shaping* spoke to the deepest questions of my heart and brought to the surface issues that have been hindering my walk with God. It helped me see God's loving hands at work over the whole course of my life, good times and bad. God is using it to heal hurts and resolve doubts that have been troubling me for years. Thanks so much for this excellent material."

Susan Nikaido, former editor of *Discipleship Journal*

"Let *Soul Shaping* influence your 'being' the way *Experiencing God* guided your 'doing.' This workbook is so well crafted that you can start with any module which fits your need and experience life-defining moments."

Bill Thrall, Bruce McNicol, John Lynch, coauthors of
TrueFaced, The Ascent of a Leader, Beyond Your Best

"*Soul Shaping* is an exceptional tool for exploring the mysterious way in which God actually transforms our inner world so that Christ is seen through the cracked pots of our lives. Practical, well-grounded, immensely creative—*Soul Shaping* will be the best guide you've picked up in a long time."

Paula Rinehart, author of *Strong Women, Soft
Hearts* and *Sex and the Soul of a Woman*

"Stephen Smith has offered a tremendous gift. *Soul Shaping: A Practical Guide for Spiritual Transformation* brilliantly illuminates the truth that having our soul shaped is not about proficiency; it's about intimacy. *Soul Shaping* offers a way for those of us who want to live differently to stop our thrashing about trying to fix ourselves and simply surrender our misshapen lives into the reforming hands of the God who is hopelessly in love with us."

Fil Anderson, author of *Running On Empty:
Contemplative Spirituality for Overachievers*

"Sometimes it seems impossible to get from here to there. We've learned that a change in our circumstances is not the answer, though we might wish for it. We sense that something is calling us to be changed on the inside, but we haven't a clue how it will happen. We strive and try harder to change, only to be disappointed. There must be a more true alternative to living this way. *Soul Shaping* is a guide into true living. It is not a tool to cause change, but rather it is a help in recognizing the strong and tender hand of God already at work in us. This kind and incisive journey will free you to see the transformation that is possible—that already is happening—in you."

Jan Meyers, author of *The Allure of Hope* and *Listening to Love*

"Biblically deep, artistically rich, personally challenging, and user friendly, *Soul Shaping* by Steve Smith is the finest resource I have seen for the serious pursuit of personal transformation. If you desire to be formed by the loving hands of the Master Potter, this is your guide for becoming moldable clay."

Howard Baker, author of *Soul Keeping*, adjunct professor of spiritual formation, Denver Seminary

"Souls are created and shaped by God, who uses any means He chooses to empower the process. At times He uses souls that are in the process already to aid in the task for others. As you engage the work of soul shaping presented in this study, you enter life as experienced by the author Steve Smith—a man 'in the process.' Join him and be shaped with one whose life is on the wheel and who knows the shaping work of the Potter's hands."

Dr. Donovan Graham, World Harvest

"*Soul Shaping* by Steve Smith is a life-changing resource for every Christ-follower. This tool provides a life-transforming study of Scripture, penetrating reflection exercises, and a practical, grace-filled approach to personal application. It serves us well as either a personal study guide or for use in the context of a small group community."

Bruce Hayes, Reynolda Presbyterian Church, Winston Salem, NC

"Steve and Gwen Smith, and their calling to The Potter's Inn, are a breath of fresh air in a stale world. The prophetic cry of The Potter's Inn to deeper transformation of the soul is so vital in today's world, yet oh, so neglected. Their call to a reflective life enriched by intimate conversations with God is leading many to insight, wisdom, and invigorating life-changes. I continue to be amazed at how God has uniquely equipped this couple for this ministry—as well as their depth of insight and wealth of experiences."

Dr. Steve Sweatman, president and CEO of Missionary Training International, Monument, CO

"I have always wanted to be able to teach the Bible like a counselor, and Steve Smith's *Soul Shaping* has given me a resource for doing so. With the careful hands of a skilled surgeon of the soul, Steve Smith lays open the human heart and applies powerful and insightful principles from the Scripture. I am pleased to commend this study to those interested in seeing Scripture change lives."

J. D. Greear, PhD, senior pastor of the Summit Church, Durham, NC

"*Soul Shaping* is a biblical, holistic, timely, and timeless gift to anyone who desires a refreshing touch from the Master's hand. *Soul Shaping* is priceless!"

Clarence Shuler, author, speaker, and founder of Building Lasting Relationships

"In *Soul Shaping*, Steve Smith has created a guide to help followers of Christ enter into deeper intimacy with Jesus. This guide is a welcome departure from the 'Get the right knowledge in order to make the "right" decisions' approach to the life of faith. It is like a long walk with a wise, old friend. *Soul Shaping* helps you remember that God is crazy about you, and that He can be trusted."

Tim Pynes, Denver, CO

Soul Shaping

Soul Shaping

A PRACTICAL GUIDE
FOR SPIRITUAL TRANSFORMATION

STEPHEN W. SMITH

David C Cook®
transforming lives together

SOUL SHAPING
Published by David C Cook
4050 Lee Vance View
Colorado Springs, CO 80918 U.S.A.

David C Cook Distribution Canada
55 Woodslee Avenue, Paris, Ontario, Canada N3L 3E5

David C Cook U.K., Kingsway Communications
Eastbourne, East Sussex BN23 6NT, England

David C Cook and the graphic circle C logo
are registered trademarks of Cook Communications Ministries.

Unless otherwise noted, Scripture quotations are taken from *THE MESSAGE*. Copyright © by Eugene H.
Peterson 1993, 1994, 1995, 1996, 2000, 2001, 2002. Used by permission of NavPress Publishing Group. Scripture
quotations marked AB are taken from *The Amplified Bible*. Copyright © 1954, 1958, 1962, 1964, 1965, 1987 by
The Lockman Foundation. Used by permission; CEV are taken from the *Contemporary English Version* © 1995
by American Bible Society. Used by permission; KJV are taken from the King James Version of the Bible. (Public
Domain.); NIV are taken from the Holy Bible, New International Version®, NIV®. Copyright © 1973, 1978, 1984
by Biblica, Inc™. Used by permission of Zondervan. All rights reserved worldwide. www.zondervan.com; NKJV
are taken from the New King James Version. Copyright © 1982 by Thomas Nelson, Inc. Used by permission.
All rights reserved; NLT are taken from the New Living Translation of the Holy Bible. New Living Translation
copyright © 1996, 2004 by Tyndale Charitable Trust. Used by permission of Tyndale House Publishers.

ISBN 978-0-7814-0454-9
eISBN 978-0-7814-0596-6

© 2011 Stephen W. Smith

The Team: John Blase, Amy Kiechlin, Erin Prater, Karen Athen
Cover Design: John Lucas Design
Cover Photo: iStockphoto

Printed in the United States of America
First Edition 2011

1 2 3 4 5 6 7 8 9 10

110510

For Austin and Harrison Doyle, my two godsons and every other child of God who will want to know how they were shaped, why they were shaped, and who it is that is still shaping them throughout their lives.

CONTENTS

ACKNOWLEDGMENTS

Many hands and souls have helped shape my own understanding of spiritual formation and how a person really transforms through Jesus Christ. There are far too many to list here.

I am mindful of teachers, aunts, uncles, cousins, friends, pastors, leaders, and soul advocates who shaped my soul as a young boy growing up in North Carolina. Through each hand—strong or tender, I now realize they were God's pursuit to shape me.

Here I want to acknowledge Judy Couchman who helped me conceptualize this guidebook. Judy's expertise in coaching me, assisting me, and shaping this guidebook has been invaluable. I am very grateful.

The David C Cook team has been a champion and advocate of my message. I want to thank Don Pape for believing in this project and seeing it through to completion. John Blase, Jack Campbell, and Amy Kiechlin have all helped this guide come into existence through the David C Cook family.

Soul Shaping and the message of spiritual formation are the core and foundation of the ministry of Potter's Inn. The timeless image of the potter and clay and our shaping journey is critical to help people understand their own story of spiritual formation. I'm convinced this is why this image is in the Bible so many times.

ABOUT THIS PRACTICAL GUIDE

Listed below are descriptions of the activities featured in the eight sessions of *Soul Shaping*. Each session was designed with reading, study, reflection, prayer, and application in mind. Many of the lessons incorporate classic spiritual disciplines that will help you experience God and His transformational hands in a deep, soulful way.

This practical guide is meant to be a resource during your spiritual-formation journey. You can pick and choose based on what is helpful to you, what learning style works best for you, and how you best experience God's shaping hands in your life. You can go at your own pace. You don't have to finish a session in one sitting or even in one week. It may take you several different settings to work through a session. Small-group facilitators and class leaders can choose the activities that work for their class and assign other activities as homework.

 Introduction

A brief narrative that introduces each section and gives you an overview of the topics you'll be exploring.

 The Potter's Heart

The Bible-study section. Here you will explore passages and verses that engage your mind and heart as you consider, study, and investigate what God is saying. Some passages you'll explore in-depth. Others you'll be asked to look up and interact with. These provide opportunities to become familiar with and consider God's Word and the responses of biblical figures to these themes.

A Potter's Work

A sample of Christian poetry, quotes, or lyrics—a way for you to become familiar with what other people have said on this subject.

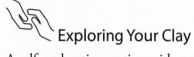 ## Exploring Your Clay

A self-exploration section with activities that let you apply the session's topic and themes. Additional worksheets provide additional study, reflection, and exercises.

 ## Soul Impressions

Allows you to examine what you learned in the previous section through questions, activities, journaling, and other methods. You'll be prompted to reflect more deeply on feelings, soulful issues, or struggles related to the session's theme.

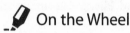 ## On the Wheel

A life-application section. How will you apply the lesson's principles to life? How will you allow God to work? How will you take steps in this direction?

 ## Prayers to the Potter

A creative prayer guide related to the session's topic. One might offer a prayer to read, another might encourage writing a prayer, another might encourage praying Bible verses or practicing Scripture meditation. The prayer activity concludes the session.

 ## Notes for the Journey

Quotes from great Christians and intellectuals. The quotes focus on the session's theme.

 ## Additional Resources

Helpful suggestions and additional readings are suggested in each section and in the back of the workbook.

The Ancient Art of Soul Shaping

The art of spiritual formation has recently reemerged after years of neglect. Theologian and author Dallas Willard notes that the concept "was understood by Jesus, taught by Paul, obeyed by the early church, followed with excess in the medieval church, narrowed by the reformers, recaptured by the Puritans, and virtually lost in the modern church."[1] But we can regain the ground we've lost. We can explore the ancient faith practices of our spiritual ancestors and follow them into a deeper relationship with God.

As we learn to walk with God as Jesus did, we embrace the delight of a Father-child relationship. We uncover the pain, failings, and addictions in our lives. We acknowledge our need for transformation. We begin to desire change, to desire something more, something better. Thankfully, God meets us at our point of need and lovingly guides us through the lifelong process of spiritual transformation.

The timeless image of a potter's hands creatively shaping clay serves as a poignant allegory of God's work in our souls—one of the most powerful scriptural pictures of spiritual transformation. In Genesis, God scoops clay from the ground and forms a human. Job uses the pottery metaphor to express his consternation with God. He says, "You made me like a handcrafted piece of pottery—and now are you going to smash me to pieces?" (Job 10:9–10). Both Jeremiah and Isaiah use the metaphor to explain God's ways with His people: The passionate Creator commits to shaping a nation until its people walk in His ways. Isaiah's straightforward confession forms a preamble for our transformation journey. He writes, "We're the clay and you're our potter; all of us are what you made us" (Isa. 64:8).

In the New Testament, this same image proves valuable to Paul as he admonishes the early Christians. Paul says, "Who in the world do you think you are to second-guess God? Do you for one moment suppose any of us knows enough to call God into question? Clay doesn't talk back to the fingers that mold it, saying, 'Why did you shape me like this?' Isn't it obvious that a potter has a perfect right to shape one lump of clay into a vase for holding flowers and another into a pot for cooking beans?" (Rom. 9:20–22). When describing our fragile and sometimes broken lives, Paul says we are "jars of clay" that God's glory might shine through (2 Cor. 4:7 NIV). This is the meaning and work of spiritual transformation.

Getting Below the Surface

The prophet Jeremiah's encounter with a working potter forms the foundation of this study of spiritual transformation (Jer. 18:1–7). While in the potter's house, Jeremiah sees something deeper than pottery-making going on—something deeper, something spiritual. This soul-stirring image becomes the vehicle for his transformational message to Israel. We will use the potter-clay metaphor to "get beyond our minds" and experience transformation at an authentic, below-the-surface level. The potter metaphor also provides a common language to dialogue, connect with one another, and refine our understanding of this spiritual process. This compelling image offers a way to frame our individual stories.

As we examine and tell our stories, we can remember these guidelines.

- **God deals with each of us uniquely.** No two life stories or transformation processes look the same. The Divine Potter shapes each of us differently over time. Consequently, there is no exact formula for transformation. God considers our background, personality, needs, wounds, strengths, weaknesses, and the other elements that form our clay. He accordingly shapes us into a one-of-a-kind vessel fit for spiritual use, endurance, and enjoyment. Still, the potter-clay metaphor spotlights the transformational principles that we all share.

- **We decide whether we'll sit on the Potter's wheel.** We can either face the moving wheel with acceptance and courage, knowing that God's hands hold us, or we can shrink back, resentful of the Potter's hands and cynical about His intention. We can sit on the wheel and welcome change or we can stay the same primitively formed lump of clay that can't endure the fire. Hopefully we choose to sit on the Potter's wheel.

  In God the Potter's hands, we find the promise of hope over failure, beginnings in the face of adversity, and life emerging from the ashes. We discover the true gospel. God uses our past. Nothing is discarded. Everything is available to mold us into authentic individuals, and we're able to anticipate how God will meaningfully shape our future.

- **Spiritual transformation is a process and a journey.** Spiritual transformation is not rigid expectations and requirements. It is an ongoing process—more fluid and open-ended than a set of rules—filled with grace and hope. The lengthy process involves repeated opportunities to understand the command to "taste and see that the LORD is good" (Ps. 34:8 KJV). We don't just get one chance to learn. The Potter extends repeated invitations to grow and change. There are many variable factors and forays into the unknown. In this regard spiritual transformation becomes a journey. While the final destination is important on any journey, there is more to a trip than just "getting there." Along the way we learn what is valuable.

    In their remarkable book *The Critical Journey: Stages of Life and Faith*, Janet Hagberg and Robert Geulich remind us of the importance of the journey: "A journey involves process, action, movement, change, experiences, stops and starts, variety, humdrum, and surprises. For us a journey implies more than a quick trip from point A to point B. It is more extended, with the time and place between departure and final destination being important for their own sake."[2]

- **We can surrender and trust.** Spiritual transformation is about surrendering to the Potter. It is about becoming aware of God's ways and His compassionate heart toward us. It is about releasing our demands. It is about accepting the Potter, trusting His hands, and relaxing in the process. In turn, we learn our role and how to collaborate with Him. We discover our purpose. We craft a better life. We join in the chorus of rejoicing Christians who have traveled ahead of us. We transform.

A Guide for the Journey

Soul Shaping is a guide to this amazing journey. It is anchored in Scripture and filled with exercises to guide spiritual transformation. In these pages you'll look backward and forward, inward and outward. You'll remember the past and dream about the future. It is an invitation to see yourself as you really are and imagine who you can become. But most of all, it is an opportunity to change by trusting the Potter's work in your life.

I would encourage you to move with intentionality and great flexibility through *Soul Shaping*. Not everything in this workbook will fit your circumstances, but I hope the sessions will enhance your journey. I am not the Potter; only He can be your all-knowing guide. I can only say, "Welcome to the Potter's studio. A great work has begun."

Soul Journey

Choosing the path of spiritual transformation

In our life journey, we reach places where we crave transformation—
not superficial change, but deep inner work that penetrates the
heart. That's when the Potter beckons us to visit His house.

Soul Journey

The process is the end. It is the process,
not the end, that is glorifying to God.
—*Oswald Chambers*, My Utmost for His Highest

Spiritually, are you searching for something more? Do you feel stuck in your life and don't know how to change? Are the things you've believed and wanted not working for you any longer? Take heart. You're ready for the journey of spiritual transformation.

Spiritual transformation is a process by which Christians mature and change to more fully conform to God's ideal. This spiritual growth process is a developmental one because changes occur over time. While some of these transitions are dramatic and spontaneous, most are often quiet and gradual. The goal is that our soul, character, and actions shape into the likeness of Christ. Along the way we discard the sins, habits, and other barriers to spiritual growth and maturity.

Spiritual transformation occurs as we intentionally nurture our relationship with God. There are no shortcuts to cultivating our souls. Like a potter shaping clay into a beautiful vessel, spiritual transformation requires time, attention, and patience. In fact, pottery-making is one of the most frequently used metaphors in the Bible. The image of a potter shaping clay is deeply rooted in the Old Testament. In ancient times God's people were familiar with potters and their process. Potters created both liturgical and everyday vessels, and most Jews would have observed their creative hands at work. True to His creative nature, God uses the potter metaphor to describe His work in each of us. According Isaiah 64:8 (NIV), "We are the clay, you are the potter; we are all the work of your hand."

"The environment in which pots are created is of fundamental importance: the potter must be able to concentrate in a comfortable situation, with tools and materials near to hand, together with a sympathetic ambience to suit the individual. The primary aim should be to make the circumstances conducive to the production of good work. The characteristics of a studio can be inspirational, the mood determined by the materials and sounds that prevail."
— *Alex McErlain,* Art of Throwing

As the Divine Potter shapes each of us individually, He employs a crucial process that's recognizable to us all. Each phase becomes visible in the potter metaphor. This analogy helps us grasp the concept of spiritual transformation in a deeper, more soulful way. It also provides us with a common language that allows us to dialogue, connect to one another, and refine our understanding of God's work in us. This compelling image of a potter offers us a way to frame our spiritual stories.

Though our individual stories are unique, God generally moves us through these pottery-making phases to transform us in similar ways. In this session, consider the components of the ancient art of pottery-making—the process in which the potter molds the clay with his hands—and how they relate to ongoing spiritual transformation.

♥ The Potter's Heart
A VISIT TO THE POTTER'S HOUSE

God sent Jeremiah on a mission. It was not a preaching junket. It was an assignment to become curious about, observe, and reflect on a potter's work. As Jeremiah entered the potter's workplace, he observed the process of clay being formed, reformed, and transformed. This helped the prophet to see beyond the physical into the spiritual. God invited Jeremiah to look with the eyes of his heart, and this observation led to the truth about authentic transformation.

What was the potter doing? Why was it important for Jeremiah to encounter this image? At the potter's house Jeremiah gained insight about how God works. Jeremiah's curiosity and reflection helped him become more self-aware, more in touch with what God was accomplishing in his life and the destiny of Israel. As the clay was transformed, so was Jeremiah.

In this section, become a Jeremiah. Be curious. Reflect on the pottery metaphor and how it represents spiritual transformation.

1. Read about Jeremiah's visit to the potter's house in Jeremiah 18:1–6. Why did the Lord send him to visit the potter?

   _____

   _____

   _____

2. When Jeremiah entered the house, he viewed the potter at work. Jeremiah probably used his senses as he observed the process. In the space below, describe what Jeremiah probably sensed. Use your five senses to imagine the scene.

   • What did he see?

   _____

   • What did he smell?

   _____

• What did he hear?

_____

• What did he touch?

_____

• What did he taste?

_____

3. What happened to the marred clay in the potter's hands?

_____

4. What transformation occurred in the potter's house?

_____

5. What might Jeremiah have concluded about the potter and the clay?

_____

6. What is God specifically doing in your life?

_____

Understanding how God works can assist and encourage us through the process of spiritual transformation. God knows our need for change and desires to accompany us through that process. But first we need to articulate our need for transformation—to ourselves, and then to God.

Exploring Your Clay
THE NEED TO CHANGE

When we're in need of change and recovery, God invites us to Himself. Wherever we are, whatever we've done, however we feel, God the Divine Potter yearns to tenderly guide us through spiritual transformation.

It's hard to express to God what we don't understand ourselves. So first examine your need for change and how you feel about it. Turn to Worksheet 1—"Are You Ready for Change?"—on page 35. Read about some characteristics of people who want to change and compare your desire to theirs. Then privately articulate your own feelings about needing to change.

After considering your need, explore the process of spiritual transformation. When you ask God for change, it helps to understand what's ahead.

A Potter's Work
THE TRANSFORMATION PROCESS

Spiritual transformation resembles the art of pottery-making. God is the Potter. We are the clay. To change us from a lump of clay into a gleaming vessel, the Potter's hands must guide us through the following process. You'll explore these life-changing stages in the upcoming sessions.

- **Formation (session four).** The Potter examines the clay's form before shaping it. He considers its composition and need for amendment. God begins forming us in the womb. This form includes the body, mind, heart, and soul—all that creates unique individuals. We can celebrate who God created us to be, both the strengths and weaknesses. We bring all of ourselves to the transformation process. We understand, accept, and appreciate God's shaping hands in our lives, past and present.

- **Reformation (session five).** If the clay mars or slumps during the pottery-making process, the Potter presses it down, squeezes the mass, and reshapes the form. He rebuilds the imperfect clay into something different, even better. We bring our marred lives to God, and He begins to reform us with personal wholeness and godly character in mind. He reclaims and uses our mistakes and misfortunes in the spiritual transformation process.

- **Transformation (session six).** The word *transformation* combines the Latin prefix *trans-* ("over") with the English word *formation*. Just as a potter's hands come over the clay to form it, God hovers over us. He brings mercy and change to our failures and disappointments. The Divine Potter's work in us produces gain instead of loss, beauty instead of ashes. Under the Potter's hands, we realize that spiritual transformation depends upon God—not us.

- **Conformation (session eight).** The finished vessel conforms to what the Potter envisioned when He placed His hands on the clay. The word *conform* means "to give the same form to; to make similar."[1] As we grow spiritually we desire to be like Jesus. Through the spiritual transformation process, God conforms us to His Son's image. He shapes us into who He had in mind from the beginning, before we were born.

About Your Process

1. At what stage, if any, are you in the spiritual transformation process?

_____

_____

_____

2. How do you feel about the process?

_____

_____

_____

3. Do you have any concerns or fears about the process? If so, what are they?

_____

_____

_____

Soul Impressions
YOUR HEART, GOD'S HANDS

Spiritual transformation is about changing from the heart—from the inside out. We place ourselves like clay in God's hands so He can mold us. We visit the Potter's house with the anticipation of renewal and reformation. Learn more about God the Potter and His transforming process by completing this section.

1. Read "The Transformation Process" on page 28. To consider your relationship to this process, answer the questions at the end of the excerpt.

2. Also read "Pottery-making Images for the Spiritual Life" on page 33 Answer those questions too.

3. What questions do you have about the transformation process? If these questions aren't answered in the course of this study, how can you seek out answers to them?

_____

_____

_____

Even though we want spiritual transformation, it can intimidate us. When confessing our need to change, we might fear criticism, rejection, and punishment. But the Potter's house is a safe place—a place we can rest, unburden ourselves, and safely open our hearts to change. Spiritual transformation does not occur in a vacuum. God uses people, places, events, and encounters to shape us. In the next section, think about the safe place you need for examining your life and inviting the Potter to change you.

On the Wheel
IN SEARCH OF A SAFE PLACE

Where is the heavenly Potter's house, the place for spiritual transformation? Is it an actual physical location or simply a state of mind?

Turn to Worksheet 2—"Finding a Safe Place"—on page 37. It will help you decide the nature of a supportive place for your spiritual transformation.

Then, with the prayer in the next section, commit yourself to finding a safe place of transformation.

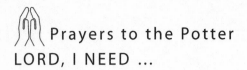 **Prayers to the Potter**

LORD, I NEED ...

In the space below, create a brief prayer that tells God about your need to change, what you need from Him, and your need for a safe place as you embark on the spiritual transformation journey. You can use the following fill-in-the-blank prayer or write your own.

Dear God,
I need to change, especially in the area(s) of ...

_____

_____

_____

I need your help with ...

_____

_____

_____

To transform with your help, I need a place that is ...

_____

_____

_____

I would also like to say that ...

_____

_____

_____

Amen.

Notes for the Journey
POTTERY-MAKING IMAGES FOR THE SPIRITUAL LIFE

Many pottery-making images apply to the spiritual journey. These comparisons can assist your understanding of the transformation process.

- **Potter.** God is the Potter who works with love, purpose, and intention. The Potter is creative, not static; involved, not detached; yearning for something more, not content with the status quo. He envisions the beautiful art form He wants to create.

- **Clay.** We are the clay. Soft and pliable clay holds possibilities for beauty and practical use. All clay is unique and bears the *imago Dei,* the mark of its Creator.

- **Wheel.** Clay on the wheel engages in a circular—not linear—transformation. The Potter guides the direction. As the clay whirls around, it's not a meaningless process. The movement allows us to examine, gain new insights, and focus on transformation.

- **Hands.** The Potter lovingly touches the clay with His hands, giving it individual attention. The action of His hands extends from His mind and heart. Without the Potter's touch, the clay would only spin and splatter, instead of taking form and finding purpose.

- **Water.** The water, often a symbol of the Holy Spirit, freshens and softens hard clay. Poured or dripped onto the clay, it creates malleability, renewal, and possibilities.

- **Process.** Pottery-making is a time-consuming process. It's also an ancient process, still practiced in time-honored ways. Spiritual transformation takes time and satisfies a yearning to connect with enduring principles.

- **Drying.** The formed clay rests and dries before firing can begin. God the Potter waits, knowing this time is crucial to the process. At times in the spiritual journey, it seems like nothing is happening. Or we feel distant, removed from the process and the shaping hands. The Potter knows that even drying times have purpose.

• **Kiln.** The kiln's fire and heat bonds shaped clay into permanent and useful vessels. The fires of life and the furnace of transformation we enter from time to time bring deep and lasting change. We become "vessels unto honor" (2 Tim. 2:21–22 KJV).

About Your Life

1. Can you think of any images to add to this list? If so, jot them down to share with your study group.

_____

_____

_____

2. Which pottery-making image do you like or identify with the most? Why?

_____

_____

_____

3. Which image do you dislike? Why?

_____

_____

_____

Worksheet One
ARE YOU READY FOR CHANGE?

Reaching the end of willpower. Though our journeys are unique, people ripe for spiritual transformation share some common feelings based on repeated attempts and failures to change on their own. Read through these statements and decide whether or not they describe you. If you're uncertain, briefly explain why. After contemplating these statements, write a brief summary about your current need for change.

1. I deeply long for change, but the formulas and seminars haven't worked. *Translation:* I am tired of tips and techniques.

   ☐ Yes   ☐ Sometimes   ☐ No

   _____

   _____

   _____

2. I want to change, but transformation requires more than human willpower. *Translation:* I finally realize that making a resolution—turning over a new leaf—only lasts with God's help.

   ☐ Yes   ☐ Sometimes   ☐ No

   _____

   _____

   _____

3. I have a pattern of repeated attempts to change, but they result in failure. *Translation:* When I have the courage to look inside my heart, I recognize persistent patterns of trying and failing.

   ☐ Yes   ☐ Sometimes   ☐ No

   _____

_____

_____

4. I have mixed feelings deep inside my heart. I want to change, yet I don't want to change. *Translation:* Couldn't I just do this a little longer? One more time?

☐ Yes   ☐ Sometimes   ☐ No

_____

_____

_____

5. Living in a state of quiet desperation, I feel hopeless. *Translation:* I don't want to be found out. After all, I have my pride and dignity.

☐ Yes   ☐ Sometimes   ☐ No

_____

_____

_____

6. This is how I currently feel about my need to change:

_____

_____

_____

Worksheet Two
FINDING A SAFE PLACE

Where can you go? We all need a "Potter's house"—a place where we can pull aside and assess our lives. When we embark on spiritual transformation, it serves as a place to rest, think, and commit ourselves to the process. Becoming curious and reflecting on God's work in our lives can happen in varied places. Moses encountered God on the backside of a mountain. David explored the work of God in pastures and caves. Jesus visited lonely places to do His soul work. Jesus knew that something happens in lonely places that does not happen in places filled with people.

But spiritual transformation is an extended process, and we can't hide away indefinitely. Even if we escape for a few days to think, we also need an ongoing safe place to visit as the process continues. This might be a small group, a spiritual director, a quiet church, a chair at home, or long walks that include time to be alone with God.

Both short- and long-term places grow sacred when we meet God there. He uses these places to open our eyes to the truth about ourselves that we don't see in the daily bustle of life. But eventually these places that seem safe and sacred become more a state of being than an actual location. We learn to grow aware of God's shaping work anywhere, at any time, with anyone. We learn to open our eyes to the ever-present process of spiritual transformation. Read the following insight. Then consider what sacred places you can create during your change process.

> *Something happened to Jeremiah when he visited the potter's house, the place*
> *of transformation. He saw more than pots being formed. He heard more than*
> *the whirling potter's wheel. He felt more than the moist, soft clay. God invited*
> *Jeremiah to visit this particular place so he could see beyond the physical realm,*
> *hear beyond his human ears, and be touched with indelible markings on his*
> *soul. Jeremiah emerged from the potter's house a changed person. He awakened*
> *to deeper truths that affected his life, but also the nation of Israel.*

God often uses specific places to speak to and transform us. These are sacred places. Robert Hamma in *Landscapes of the Soul*, says, "Sacred places are valued for their 'thinness.' In them, the divine becomes transparent."[2] A sacred place can be anywhere—a mountain stream, an urban cathedral, a wooded area, a prayer closet—that opens us up to God. Paul prayed for this eye-opening experience in Ephesians 1:18 (NIV): "I pray also that the eyes of your heart may be enlightened in order that you may know the hope to which he has called you." This is the power of a sacred place.

1. In what specific places have you experienced God?

_____

_____

_____

2. What place, person, or group could become your safe place during the ongoing process of spiritual transformation?

_____

_____

_____

3. How can the places of transformation you've experienced become more of an ongoing state of being?

_____

_____

_____

You Are the Beloved

Embracing your everlasting value to the Potter

The Lord says you are His Beloved. But do you really believe it? Embracing your value to God creates an unshakable foundation for spiritual transformation. People change when they are irrevocably loved and accepted.

You Are the Beloved

Once I have accepted the truth that I am God's beloved child, unconditionally loved, I can be sent into the world to speak and to act as Jesus did.
—*Henri Nouwen,* Life of the Beloved

When we're ready for spiritual transformation—to place ourselves on the Potter's wheel—we're eager to get started—to move things along as quickly as possible. But any type of personal change requires time and needs to be founded on a solid base. For Christians, that foundation is God's love. If we don't believe in and trust His love for us, we falter and question the ongoing transformation process.

Authentic, dependable love is a divine commodity—it is not something we produce. The Bible says "love comes from God" (1 John 4:7 NIV). God embodies love. It's what He does. He offers this love to us without reserve or limitation. When we embrace this love, we believe in His goodness, concern, and involvement with us. This sounds easy. But accepting this love is actually challenging for us. For various reasons, we throw up barriers, misunderstand God's intentions, or get so busy we lose our love relationship with Him.

"If we want to deal with God the right way," writes theologian Eugene Peterson, "we have to learn to love the right way. God and love can't be separated."[1] Neither can God's love and spiritual transformation. In this session you'll explore the nature of God's love and how sacred love can transform your life.

♥ The Potter's Heart
FALLING IN LOVE AGAIN

For one to have become a Christian without having heard about God's love is unthinkable. In fact, many people accept Christ as Savior because they're compelled by God's compassion. It's a love that sacrifices His Son to forgive humanity's sins, a love that promises to follow us throughout life. Yet somewhere along the way, we can lose touch with this love, hide from its acceptance, or discover we never fully grasped it in the first place.

Eventually we can learn to separate God and love. When we face disappointment after disappointment, a gulf widens between our minds and souls. We stand on a precipice, faintly remembering a God who loves, but living a life that hurts. We secretly think God no longer loves us or that maybe He loves everyone else, but not us. So why should we love Him? Why should we trust Him, as the Potter, to mold and reshape us?

> "[Pots] are shaped not on a wheel but by hands;
> their surface texture has the faint striations of
> human skin. When you put your hand against
> my pots you are palm to palm with the artist."[2]
> —*Nadine Gordimer,* African Earth

As in other relationships that crumble from neglect or disillusionment, we can fall in love with God again—perhaps for the very first time! We can pray for a soul renewal that recognizes His unfaltering love and our value to Him. But we also need to act, to reach through the spiritual fog for what He extends to us. "The spiritual life requires a constant claiming of our true identity," said Henri Nouwen. "Our true identity is that we are God's children, the beloved sons and daughters of our heavenly Father."[3]

Understanding and living in God's love takes time. It usually doesn't happen overnight. But you can begin rekindling the flame by opening the Bible and reading about God's love for you. You'll discover that unlike people and their fickle feelings, He's never faltered in His magnificent love for you.

1. According to Ephesians 1:4, when did God choose us in love? (If possible, read this verse from *The Message*.)

   _____

   _____

   _____

2. Read Ephesians 3:14–21 (NIV). What is the "love that surpasses knowledge"? How does this love surpass knowledge? Describe what you mean.

   _____

   _____

   _____

3. What does it mean to be "rooted and grounded in love"?

   _____

   _____

   _____

4. How could a person experience the kind of love that Paul describes?

   _____

   _____

   _____

5. Read the following verses, and after each reference, write down words that describe the nature of God's love.

• Deuteronomy 7:9

_____

_____

_____

• Psalm 103:11, 17

_____

_____

_____

• Jeremiah 31:3

_____

_____

_____

6. God's unfailing love can affect our well-being. According to these verses, what does God's love extend to us?

• Deuteronomy 33:12

_____

_____

• Zephaniah 3:17

_____

_____

_____

• Psalm 6:4

_____

_____

_____

• 1 John 4:9–10

_____

_____

_____

7. Now turn to Matthew 3:13–17. When John baptized Jesus in the wilderness, what did God say about His Son? What do you imagine this would have meant to Jesus? To others who witnessed this?

_____

_____

_____

8. If we're God's children, we are also beloved by Him. *We are the Beloved.* If you really believed this, how would you feel? In the space below, write at least three words that would describe your feelings.

_____

_____

_____

Despite what we read in Scripture, many of us find it difficult to believe and live as though God loves us with an unlimited, everlasting love. To allow God's love to penetrate your soul, it's helpful to examine your misgivings about His relationship with you. Though it's not likely you'll resolve these love doubts immediately, it can place you on a path toward true belief. The next sections will help you ponder opinions about yourself and God's love.

A Potter's Work
THE QUIET, CALLING VOICE

That oft, gentle voice that calls me the Beloved has come to me in countless ways. My parents, friends, teachers, students and the many strangers who crossed my path have all sounded that voice in different tones. I have been cared for by many people with much tenderness and gentleness. I have been taught and instructed with much patience and perseverance.

I have been encouraged to keep going when I was ready to give up and was stimulated to try again when I failed. I have been rewarded and praised for success … but, somehow, all of the signs of love were not sufficient to convince me that I was the Beloved.

Beneath all my seemingly strong self-confidence there remained the question, "If all those who shower me with so much attention could see me and know me in my innermost self, would they still love me?" That agonizing question, rotted in my inner shadow, kept persecuting me and made me run away from the very place where the quiet voice calling me the Beloved could be heard.[4]
—*Henri Nouwen,* Life of the Beloved

About Your Response

1. How has God been calling you the Beloved? Consider people and experiences that might have communicated this message.

_____

_____

_____

2. How have you responded to God's quiet, calling voice about your belovedness?

_____

_____

_____

3. Do you identify with Nouwen's agonizing question? Why or why not?

_____

_____

_____

Exploring Your Clay
THE GLORY AND THE RUIN

Many of us empathize with Nouwen's agonizing question in the previous section. We ask, "If people really knew me—my sins, fears, attitudes, and struggles—would they still love me?" Or more desperate yet, "How could God possibly love me? How can He say I am the Beloved when I'm a strong-willed mess?"

Scripture addresses the paradox of our humanity. God says we're His delight, but we're also sinners to the core. We're endowed with both glory and ruin. It's the ruin—what Nouwen calls the "inner shadow"—that badgers us into shame, disbelief, and hiding. But God forgives our sins and wants us to grasp the glory.

1. **If you didn't read the preceding section ("The Quiet, Calling Voice"), do so now and consider how Henri Nouwen responded to God naming him the Beloved. Take time to privately answer the questions following the excerpt from his book, *Life of the Beloved*.**

2. **Turn to Worksheet 3—"The Glory and the Ruin"—on page 59 to learn how, despite our sinfulness, God still calls us the Beloved. Then answer the questions about your human contradictions and private disbelief regarding your belovedness. If you're studying this session with a group, you can still keep these notes private. Remember that there's nothing that separates you from God's love and nothing He can't forgive.**

While completing this session you might discover that your failings aren't what bother you most. Maybe you believe that God forgives you, but perhaps you can't accept who He made you to be, or your relationships, or your circumstances. "If God made me with this big nose, gave me an alcoholic father, or transferred me to this community, how could He love me?" These factors also affect our acceptance of God's love.

The next section will help you think about this, but it will also help you think about the positive aspects of your individuality.

"I want my work to have a spiritual dimension to it that offers something positive to those who handle it and use what I make. Pottery demands energy, discipline, and imagination on the part of the potter that is seen and felt in what is created. My favorite statement in Proverbs expresses the Spirit at work in the creative process: 'I was right beside the LORD, helping him plan and build. I made him happy each day and I was happy at his side' (Proverbs 8:30 CEV)."[5]

—*Roy Yoder, potter at Oakleaf Pottery*

Soul Impressions
SHAPING YOUR PERCEPTIONS

Sometimes we can't accept God's love because we don't love ourselves. Aside from our sin, we're ashamed about aspects of our soul, heritage, abilities, personality, or environment. Because our friends, family, workplace, or culture diminishes certain characteristics, so do we. Or sometimes we choose to disdain something about ourselves that nobody else notices. Humans develop a great capacity for self-criticism.

But self-perceptions can be wrong, even debilitating—especially when they reject God's view of us. The Bible says, "Long before he laid down earth's foundations, he had us in mind, had settled on us as the focus of his love, to be made whole and holy by his love" (Eph. 1:4). Because God loves us, we can love ourselves. Because God loves others, we can see the belovedness in them, too.

Turn to Worksheet 4—"What's Your Shape?"—on page 61. Use this written exercise to think about your self-perceptions, the good and not so good. As you answer the questions, remember that negative statements and feelings of unworthiness don't originate with God. You are His Beloved. He says, "I have loved you with an everlasting love; I have drawn you with loving-kindness" (Jer. 31:3 NIV). In turn, He wants you to say, "I am my beloved's, and my beloved is mine" (Song 6:3 NKJV).

1. Review the SHAPE perceptions of yourself. Circle all of the positive aspects about yourself and your life. How do you feel about these? Do they affect your acceptance of God's love for you? Why or why not?

   _____

   _____

   _____

2. Think about the SHAPE perceptions that cause you to question God's love. When you reject God's loving view of you, whose lies do you listen to? How can you deal with these lies?

   _____

   _____

   _____

Once we acknowledge our barriers to God's love, we can begin to dismantle them. It begins with looking at love in light of reality.

✐ On the Wheel
A LOOK AT LOVE AND REALITY

Often we gauge God's love for us by the circumstances in our lives. If we obtain our heart's desires, receive sufficient provision, and enjoy our surroundings, we believe that God loves us. If we're disappointed, the victim of tragedy, or dislike our appearance, then we can doubt God's love. If God loves us, why would He allow this pain? God's goodness and love seems to change according to the faulty and shifting conditions of life.

But that's not the truth. God's Word says He loves us eternally, consistently, and comprehensively. He loves us with the fervor of a lover toward his beloved and desires what's best for us. But reality is also this: We live in a fallen world, marred by sin in all aspects of life. We will not be perfect, and our surroundings will not be perfect until we reach heaven. In the meantime, God's love remains the same, longing to guide, comfort, and heal the ravages of our broken humanity.

1. Look again at the ruin and weakness that keep you from experiencing God's love. Make a list of adjectives that you feel God might use to describe you. What does your list tell you about your perceptions of yourself and how you feel God looks at you?

   _____

   _____

   _____

2. Self-condemnation and self-rejection are often lingering companions on the spiritual journey. What do you know about these two traveling companions?

   _____

   _____

   _____

3. Reconsider the items on your SHAPE worksheet that disappoint and weigh you down. Choose one or two factors. How can you begin to filter God's love into these circumstances? For example, do you need to be more open to observing what's

good? Are there things you could finally accept, thereby freeing yourself from disappointment?

_____

_____

_____

Remember

You are the Beloved whether you feel that way or not. But how much better to bask in the light of your belovedness!

Notes for the Journey
TRY SOME SOULFUL INDULGENCE

One evening while my wife and I were dining with friends at a restaurant, our waiter gave a particularly vivid description of the evening's featured entrée. "Tonight we have a wonderful, tender steak that has marinated for seven days in the rich spices of ginger and teriyaki. It's been rubbed with fresh garlic and cracked black pepper, and left to marinate in the juices of fresh Hawaiian pineapple."

The steak's description made for some meaningful conversation that night. We noted the waiter's word choice. While steaks marinate, people do not. We're too busy. We push forward so we're not sidelined. We seldom stop to sit and think.

I'd like to challenge this craziness. I'm suggesting that we learn to marinate in the love of God. I propose that we indulge ourselves, even if for a few moments of each day, in the fact that we're the objects of God's affection. The artist Leonardo da Vinci said that the five senses are ministers to the soul. We can marinate in God's love through what we see, hear, smell, touch, and taste. We can creatively enjoy our loving Creator.[6]

About Your Senses

1. How can you adjust your life to marinate in God's love?

_____

_____

_____

2. In what ways can you marinate in this love?

_____

_____

_____

3. How can you awaken your senses to God's love?

_____

_____

_____

Prayers to the Potter
THE POWER OF REPETITION

Teachers understand that repetition helps people learn, especially when the concept is difficult to grasp. It can be hard for us to comprehend God's love for us as individuals. Every day for a week read the following prayer to God. It's adapted from 1 Corinthians 13:4–8, a passage about the nature of love. Speak it aloud, if possible.

Before you begin, ask God to help you soak in and perceive His love for you during the week. You could also copy this prayer on an index card and carry it with you and read it several times a day. Or memorize it. There's power in repetition.

Dear God,

Help me to soak in Your love.

Your love is patient; Your love is kind.

Your love for me is not rude. It is not self-seeking. It is not easily angered. When You forgive my sin, You keep no record of my wrongs.

Your love does not delight in evil but rejoices in the truth.

Your love protects me, trusts in me, hopes for me, and perseveres with me.

Your love never fails.

Thank You.

Amen.

Notes for the Journey
STICKING GOD'S LOVE TO THE SOUL

Velcro improves the quality of life. This unique invention offers a quick alternative to the needle and thread. It holds fabrics in place, ensures garments close properly, and keeps freestanding objects together. There are hundreds of uses for this amazing product, which saves both time and frustration.

I wish someone could invent Velcro for the soul. To live fully we need God's truths to stick *to* us and *in* us. Imagine God's sacred and holy love sticking to you, filling your soul but never leaking out of it. Believing you are the object of God's passionate affection could transform your understanding of Him, yourself, and others. Rather than clinging to self-condemnation and contempt, you could live freely, gracefully, and purposefully.

About Your Soul

1. About how much of God's love sticks to your soul now? Explain.

_____

_____

_____

2. To make room for God's love, what beliefs and habits might you need to alter?

_____

_____

_____

3. What would your life look like if God's love permanently stuck to your soul?

_____

_____

_____

Worksheet Three
THE GLORY AND THE RUIN

God's great answers. The following verses pair statements about our sin (ruin) with responses from God about our belovedness to Him (glory). Circle one verse about ruin and one verse about glory that you identify with the most. In the margins, jot down your reasons for empathy with these statements. Then turn to the back of this page and further explore your response to God's unremitting love for you. If you're in a group, have the group read these verses out loud.

Behold, I was brought forth in iniquity, and in sin my mother conceived me. (Ps. 51:5 NKJV)

Your fame went out among the nations because of your beauty, for it was perfect through My splendor which I had bestowed on you. (Ezek. 16:14 NKJV)

I am a sinful man, O Lord! (Luke 5:8 NKJV)

Behold, you are fair, my love! Behold, you are fair! (Song 4:1 NKJV)

I abhor myself, and repent in dust and ashes. (Job 42:6 NKJV)

You are all fair, my love, and there is no spot in you. (Song 4:7 NKJV)

I find then a law, that evil is present with me the one who wills to do good. (Rom. 7:21 NKJV)

Be of good cheer; your sins are forgiven you. (Matt. 9:2 NKJV)

I know that in me (that is, in my flesh) nothing good dwells. (Rom. 7:18 NKJV)

You are complete in Him. (Col. 2:10 NKJV)

[You are] perfect in Christ Jesus. (Col. 1:28 NKJV)

You were washed ... you were sanctified ... you were justified in the name of the
Lord Jesus and by the Spirit of our God. (1 Cor. 6:11 NKJV)

Do you believe you're the Beloved despite your ruin and weaknesses? Use these questions to explore your feelings. They focus on the personal failings that block us from embracing God's love.

Blocks to Belief

1. What keeps you from believing in your belovedness? Think about the sin and ruin in you and your life that causes you to hide from His love.

   _____

   _____

   _____

2. What's the glory in you and your life? List or write about what's wonderful about you—not about other people.

   _____

   _____

   _____

3. What's difficult about accepting the paradox of both the glory and ruin in you and your life? Why?

   _____

   _____

   _____

Worksheet Four
WHAT'S YOUR SHAPE?

The shape of things. Consider these influences that affect people's opinions of themselves. Can you think of others' influences? Jot them down in the appropriate space. Then turn to the back of this worksheet to examine the shape of your beliefs today.

S	*Soul*	• The center of our being. • Made in the image and likeness of God. • God's internal mark on us. • Lives eternally. • Animates and enlivens body.
H	*Heritage*	• Traits we inherit. • Our genetic makeup and physical body. • Physical predispositions. • Family of origin. • Religious and cultural influences.
A	*Abilities*	• Mental capacity, our intelligence quotient. • Multiple intelligences such as linguistic, logical/ mathematical, bodily/kinesthetic, visual/spatial, musical/rhythmic, interpersonal, intrapersonal, naturalist/spiritual. • Creative abilities and talents. • Mechanical skills. • Communication through five senses or compensation due to physical challenges.
P	*Personality*	• Aspects such as extrovert, introvert, sensing, feeling, intuiting, thinking, judging, perceiving. • Disposition. • Likes, dislikes, and individual nuances. • Emotions/feelings.
E	*Environment*	• Social interactions and friendships. • Soulful advocates and supporters. • Community and workplace. • Involvement or effects of aesthetics/beauty/arts. • Place in history, such as cultural, political, economic, climate. • Geographic place, its location and nature.

Worksheet Four
WHAT'S YOUR SHAPE?

Your self-perceptions. In this blank chart, fill in the qualities that describe your perception of yourself, both the positive and the negative. (Remember that perceptions aren't always true, but they do affect how we live.) Consult the other side of this worksheet, but you can also note factors not on those lists. How do you feel about the shape of your perceptions? You may want to write the answer on separate sheet or in a journal.

S	*Soul*	
H	*Heritage*	
A	*Abilities*	
P	*Personality*	
E	*Environment*	

Trusting the Potter's Hands

Falling into the safe and tender hands of God

The journey of spiritual transformation begins with God's hands, not ours. As He readies and works our clay, He tenderly hovers over and protects us. We can trust His intentions as He places us on His wheel.

Trusting the Potter's Hands

Let us fall into the hand of the LORD, for His mercies are great.

—*2 Samuel 24:14 NKJV*

Tenderness. It's an important quality for a potter who handles clay. A potter's hands guide and coax the clay toward transformation, and rough handling can collapse the developing vessel. In pottery-making as well as in spiritual transformation, the final outcome depends on attentive, careful hands.

> "If you take some time to explore pottery and sculpture with your hands, closing your eyes so that you can rediscover your tactile sense, you will find that such exploration can bring a new perspective and new vitality to your clay forms. Your hands are an extension not only of your arms but of your whole body—indeed, of your entire being. It is that being, that individuality, that will give a pot or a sculpture its expressive quality, for clay captures not only the imprint of the maker's fingers but also the imprint of human creativity."[1]
> —*Charlotte F. Speight and John Toki,* Hands in Clay

The journey of spiritual transformation begins with God's hands, not ours. Only God can transform our clay. He places us on His whirling pottery wheel, leans over, and shapes us. We bring ourselves to the Potter, but we can't control the work of His hands. It's our part to trust His process and to relax in His hands so we're pliable and responsive.

But it's difficult to trust if we're not familiar with the Potter's character, nature, and the intent of His hands. Rembrandt van Rijn's famous baroque painting, *The Return of the Prodigal,* offers a creative insight to God's hands.[2] The painting illustrates the prodigal son returning home and kneeling in front of his forgiving father. The wayward son's bowed, shaven head leans on his father's chest against the old man's heart. In turn, the father's hands rest upon his son's bent shoulders.

Looking at the painting, our eyes rest on the father's hands, the focal point of the composition. The hands appear dramatically dissimilar. One hand looks strong, masculine, and slightly short. The other hand looks smooth, sensitive, and graceful. Through the hands, Rembrandt captured the father's heart as strong and loving, firm and forgiving.

The painter also captures the heart and hands of God. In the parable of the prodigal son, the father represents God, who extends strength and tenderness to His children. As the Potter, God works our clay with these same qualities in His hands.

In this session you'll consider the nature of God's hands and how to trust their good intentions for you.

♥ The Potter's Heart
A STRONG AND TENDER TOUCH

Just as we're compelled to look toward the father's hands in Rembrandt's painting, we're drawn toward the hands of God in our lives. We want their blessing and comfort, care and provision. We could wonder instead if His hands will hurt or ignore us. Throughout our lives we wrestle with two questions about God's hands: "Are they good?" and "Can I trust them?" Studying the nature of God's hands in Scripture can encourage us to answer these questions with a confident *yes*.

1. Read Psalm 62:11–12. What are the two characteristics that David uses to describe God?

_____

_____

_____

It might seem incongruous that God is both strong and loving. Our culture can equate loving qualities with weakness. God models that strength and tenderness can coexist and complement one another. Love can be powerful and strength can be gentle. In turn, strength and love direct the intent of God's heart and the actions of His hands. In the next questions consider the strength of God's hands and what they bring to the clay on the Potter's wheel.

2. Turn to Exodus 13:3, 14–16. How is the hand of God described? What did His hand do?

_____

_____

_____

3. Read Joshua 4:20–24. Again, how is God's hand described? What did His hand do?

_____

_____

_____

4. In Job 40:9–14, God questions Job. What does this passage reveal about the arm of the Lord?

_____

_____

_____

5. Read David's grateful prayer in 1 Chronicles 29:10–14. What does he say about God's hand?

_____

_____

_____

After reading about God's strong hand, some people fear His work in their lives. But as God's children, we can remember that His hand is mighty to save and powerful to protect us. As we sit on the Potter's wheel, settled in those strong hands, it's not His intent to destroy, but to guard, hold, and heal. God also touches us with loving hands, displaying His heart of mercy and gentleness. In the next questions, explore the tenderness of God.

6. Read Exodus 34:6–7. What does Moses tell us about God's heart toward us?

_____

_____

_____

7. Read Isaiah 40:11. Isaiah describes God as a shepherd. How does the Lord hold His sheep?

_____

_____

_____

8. In Mark 10:13, 16, what does Jesus do? How do His actions reveal what's in His heart?

_____

_____

_____

9. According to the following passages, what are Christ's qualities?

   • Matthew 11:28–30

_____

_____

_____

   • 2 Corinthians 10:1

_____

_____

_____

   • Titus 3:4

_____

_____

_____

10. Read Luke 23:46. Before Jesus died, He placed Himself in God's hands despite the tragic circumstances. At that moment, it must have been difficult to trust those hands. Nobody could envision the glorious outcome ahead. At this point in your life, how do you feel about accepting the goodness of God's hands and trusting them?

_____

_____

_____

If God's nature is good, gentle, and loving, then His artistic intentions will express these qualities. The work of His hands will reflect His heart. But sometimes we don't connect this fact in our souls because other hands have treated us differently. Next, think about how human hearts and hands have affected you.

Exploring Your Clay
YOUR HISTORY IN HANDS

It's wonderful to learn that God's hands securely and lovingly hold us during the transformation process. But the humans who have touched and managed us can influence our feelings about God's hands.
Some made us feel secure and valued; others did not.

Turn to Worksheet 5—"Your History in Hands"—on page 80. Use this exercise to discern how
people and groups formed your opinion about the hands that touch you.

1. Based on this worksheet, briefly summarize your opinion about hands—the people and
   groups who have touched, directed, and even controlled your life. In other words, what's
   your conclusion about people handling your life? How have they affected your trust?

   _____

   _____

   _____

2. If you have received wounds from someone in your life through abuse, neglect, emotional distance, or some other trauma, how has this affected you thus far on your
   journey? How have you processed it?

   _____

   _____

   _____

3. How can your conclusion in question 2 affect your opinion of God's hands and how
   they'll manage you in the spiritual transformation process?

   _____

   _____

   _____

Feeling safe in the Potter's hands depends on our trust in Him. If we have "trust issues" with people, we might harbor mistrust toward God. Or we could feel uncertain about God's dependability because we're disappointed about something He didn't do for us. Have you ever stopped to ask, "Do I really trust God?" The next section helps you answer that question.

Soul Impressions
TO TRUST OR NOT TO TRUST?

Are God's hands good? Can I trust God's hands with the clay of my life? Many of our ideas about God, ourselves, and life filter through these questions. People answer differently according to their experiences.

Turn to Worksheet 6—"To Trust or Not to Trust?"—on page 84. It's a kind of "trust-o-meter" to evaluate how you currently feel about God's trustworthiness as His hands guide you on the Potter's wheel. But it also offers healing biblical truths about God's character.

1. After completing the worksheet, how would you describe your current trust in God?

_____

_____

_____

2. Why do you think your trust is currently at this level?

_____

_____

_____

The ability to trust God affects the spiritual transformation process and the overall quality of our spiritual life. Consequently, it's worth the time, prayer, and contemplation to develop our faith and trust in God—to learn to rest as clay in His hands.

A Potter's Work
MY HEART, BARREN CLAY

My unassisted heart is barren clay.
That is of its native self can nothing feed:
Of good and pious works Thou art the seed.
That quickens only where Thou sayest it may;
Unless Thou show to us Thine own true way
No man can find it; Father! Thou must lead.
—*Michelangelo Buonarroti*

About Your Clay

1. According to Michelangelo, what is the role of the barren clay?

_____

_____

_____

2. What is the role of God the Potter?

_____

_____

_____

3. What keeps you from remaining claylike on God's wheel?

_____

_____

_____

On the Wheel
BECOMING MORE LIKE CLAY

So how can you learn to trust God more, to be like pliable clay in His hands? There's not an exact answer; we travel individual paths. But we can mull over God's Word, praying that trust will seep into our hearts. We can also choose specific actions that build our confidence in the Lord's goodness and faithfulness. Choose one or more of these activities to focus on trusting God's tender hands in your life.

Return to Worksheet 6—"To Trust or Not to Trust?"—on page 84. Read each statement and look up the Bible verse that follows it. On a separate piece of paper, write out the verse and jot down any thoughts that come to mind. Use the list as a catalyst for exploring God's faithfulness and growing your trust in Him.

1. Read the Notes for the Journey section at the end of this session. It's called "The Hovering Hands of God." Answer the questions at the end. Rewrite each verse using pottery-making terms, personalizing each with personal pronouns. For example, "God keeps me as the apple of His eye, safely under His hands while I'm on the Potter's wheel." Reread these statements periodically when you need reassurance.

   _____

   _____

   _____

2. What can you do to transform any unfortunate history with hands? Revisit Worksheet 5—"Your History in Hands"—on page 80, and list a few steps you could take. Set a timeline for completion.

   _____

   _____

   _____

Prayers to the Potter
I AM IN YOUR HANDS

If you feel ready, say this prayer to God, telling Him that you're willing to trust the work of His hands in your life. Sign your name and today's date at the bottom, as a marker and reminder for your journey ahead.

> *Dear Potter,*
>
> *The lump of clay that I am keeps me crying*
> *for some form from day to day.*
> *I yearn for you to mold me.*
> *This is a trust-song, Lord.*
> *I am in your hands like clay.*
> *I am ready to be transformed.*
> *I expect to be molded.*
> *I expect to be beautiful.*
> *I expect to be loved.*
> *And if by chance someone should drop me*
> *as your apprentices sometimes do,*
> *I expect to be hurt.*
> *I am just trying to say*
> *I have surrendered to your dream for me.*
> *I am in your hands like clay.*
> *Amen.*[3]
>
> *—A Prayer to the Potter by Macrina Wiederkehr*

Your Name _____

Date _____

Notes for the Journey
THE HOVERING HANDS OF GOD

First this: God created the Heavens and Earth—all you see, all you don't
see. Earth was a soup of nothingness, a bottomless emptiness, an inky
blackness. God's Spirit brooded like a bird above the watery abyss.
—*Genesis 1:2*

The opening of Genesis describes God as brooding, hovering, and moving over a shapeless mass. Then He begins creating the beautiful earth, and everything that fills it. This is similar to the image of the Potter who uses tender, loving hands to form a lump of clay. His hands hover above and around the clay, providing safety and assurance during its formation.

Biblical writers recognized the hovering God. They likened Him to a mother bird protecting her babies, sweeping them under her wings. Contemplate these biblical metaphors about God's protective wings and how they also apply to the Potter's hands.

> *[God is] like an eagle that stirs up its nest and hovers over its young, that spreads its wings to catch them and carries them on its pinions. (Deuteronomy 32:11 NIV)*

> *May you be richly rewarded by the LORD, the God of Israel, under whose wings you have come to take refuge. (Ruth 2:12b NIV)*

> *Keep me as the apple of your eye; hide me in the shadow of your wings. (Psalm 17:8 NIV)*

> *How priceless is your unfailing love! Both high and low among men find refuge in the shadow of your wings. (Psalm 36:7 NIV)*

> *Have mercy on me, O God, have mercy on me, for in you my soul takes refuge. (Psalm 57:1a NIV)*

I will take refuge in the shadow of your wings until the disaster has passed. (Psalm 57:1b NIV)

I long to dwell in your tent forever and take refuge in the shelter of your wings. (Psalm 61:4 NIV)

Because you are my help, I sing in the shadow of your wings. (Psalm 63:7 NIV)

About Your Relationship

1. What has been your response to God's hovering hands?

_____

_____

_____

2. What are the personal benefits of staying under God's protective hands?

_____

_____

_____

3. Which verse best describes your relationship to God's hands?

_____

_____

_____

Worksheet Five
YOUR HISTORY IN HANDS

The hands that held you. Throughout our lives, we're touched by the "hands" of people in authority or in relationship with us. Through these experiences, we create an opinion about hands—what it means when other people touch and manage our lives.

1. **Think about hands that have significantly affected your life. Choose up to three, and write the name of the person or group below the hand drawings on the following pages. This could include parents, spouses, teachers, church leaders, etc.**

2. **Above the fingertips of each hand, write the characteristics of this person or group's hands. For example, on the top of the thumb you could write "gentle" or "tough." On the index finger you could write "nurturing" or "neglectful," etc.**

3. **Below the hand illustration, briefly summarize what this person or group taught you about hands, either positive, negative, or both.**

Worksheet Five
YOUR HISTORY IN HANDS

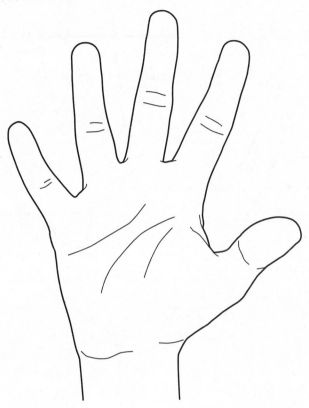

What You Learned About Hands

_____

_____

_____

Person or Group

_____

Worksheet Five
YOUR HISTORY IN HANDS

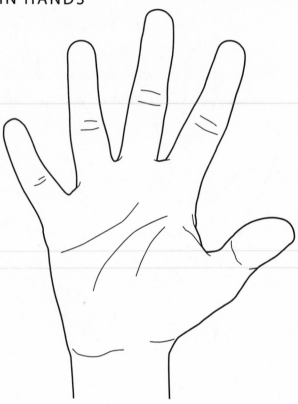

What You Learned About Hands

_____

_____

_____

Person or Group

_____

Worksheet Five
YOUR HISTORY IN HANDS

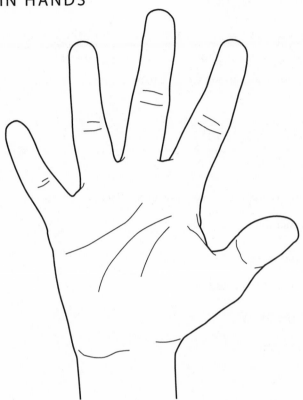

What You Learned About Hands

_____

_____

_____

Person or Group

_____

Worksheet Six
TO TRUST OR NOT TO TRUST?

A matter of trust. Indicate your honest response to each of these scriptural statements about God. Don't answer the way you think you should, but the way you feel now. At one time or another, most of us harbor doubts or questions about God's trustworthiness. So don't be hard on yourself or think you're alone.

1. God is good. (Ps. 119:68; 136:1)

☐ Yes   ☐ Sometimes   ☐ No

2. God loves me and wants me to have His best. (Rom. 8:32, 38–39)

☐ Yes   ☐ Sometimes   ☐ No

3. I am complete and accepted in Christ. (Eph. 1:3–6)

☐ Yes   ☐ Sometimes   ☐ No

4. God is enough. (Ps. 23:1)

☐ Yes   ☐ Sometimes   ☐ No

5. God can be trusted. (Isa. 28:16)

☐ Yes   ☐ Sometimes   ☐ No

6. God doesn't make mistakes. (Isa. 48:10)

☐ Yes   ☐ Sometimes   ☐ No

7. God's grace is sufficient for me. (2 Cor. 12:9)

☐ Yes   ☐ Sometimes   ☐ No

8. The blood of Christ is sufficient to cover all my sin. (1 John 1:7)

☐ Yes   ☐ Sometimes   ☐ No

9. The cross of Christ can conquer my sinful flesh. (Rom. 6:6–7)

☐ Yes   ☐ Sometimes   ☐ No

10. My past does not have to plague me. (1 Cor. 6:9–11)

☐ Yes   ☐ Sometimes   ☐ No

11. God's Word is sufficient to lead, teach, and heal me. (Ps. 19:7; 107:20; 119:105)

☐ Yes   ☐ Sometimes   ☐ No

12. Through the Holy Spirit's power, God will enable me to do anything he asks me to do. (1 Thess. 5:24)

☐ Yes   ☐ Sometimes   ☐ No

Your Fearful and Wonderful Form

Exploring the clay that shapes your uniqueness

In the journey of spiritual transformation, we are like clay in God's hands.

He's familiar with the elements of our earthly composition,
the positives and negatives that infiltrate the soul. He knows
how to turn our imperfect clay into an enduring vessel.

Your Fearful and Wonderful Form

It is absolutely crucial … to keep in constant touch
with what is going on in your own life's story.
—*Frederick Buechner*

When a potter begins to make a pot, he starts with raw, unassisted clay. His creative eyes envision a finished form in this exposed, unadorned, organic material. The artist Michelangelo said every work he sculpted began with such vision casting.

With gifted, strong, and loving hands, the Potter collaborates with His whirling wheel to shape an image that previously existed only in His mind. He works patiently and persistently to firmly shape the clay, pinching here, pulling there, until the vessel emerges. But before the Potter begins this process, He examines the clay. He wants to identify the elements that characterize this particular organic lump. He intends to understand its raw form.

Many kinds of clay exist, unearthed from deposits around the globe. An experienced potter knows that location and environment affect a clay's personality, filling it with a variety of useful and harmful particles. So once a potter understands the clay's composition, he knows its strengths and weaknesses. He ponders if the clay needs alteration and determines what those changes should be. An additive? An extraction? The potter alters the clay not on a whim, but to strengthen the emerging shape and its long-term usefulness as a vessel.

In the journey of spiritual transformation, we are like clay in God's hands. He's familiar with the elements of our earthly composition, the positives and negatives that infiltrate the soul. He knows how to turn our imperfect clay into an enduring vessel. At the same time, it's difficult to yield to the Potter's work if we don't understand the components of our clay. As we enter the Potter's house, we bring along the influences of heritage, abilities, personality, and environment—all the things beloved by the Potter, all the things that could help or hinder His creative hands.

In this session, explore your clay and how it could affect God's transformation process. Be curious about what resides in your soul. Celebrate your existing form. Then, as you approach the Potter's wheel, be confident of His creative abilities.

♥ THE POTTER'S HEART
Our Fearful and Wonderful Clay

When God created Adam, He "formed the man from the dust of the ground and breathed into his nostrils the breath of life, and man became a living being" (Genesis 2:7 NIV). These are humble beginnings. Humanity was formed from clay, the moistened dust of God's earth. Interestingly, the words *humble* and *humility* derive from the word *humus,* which means "rich earth." Humus is partially decayed organic material, rich in nutrients. Gardeners use it to aid the growth of their trees, flowers, and vegetables. As living beings that will return to the dust, we share its connection to the earth.

Most of us don't like to think of ourselves as messy lumps of clay. But God loves clay. When we remember our original composition, we make room for His glory and greatness in our lives. In this section, you will learn what the Bible says about your connection to humble clay and a great God.

1. Read the following verses. What do they reveal about our humble beginnings?

• Job 1:21

_____

_____

_____

• Ecclesiastes 3:20

_____

_____

_____

2. Consider Isaiah's response to his "clayness" in Isaiah 64:8. What is his attitude toward God the Potter?

_____

_____

_____

3. According to Paul, why do we function as clay pots? See 2 Corinthians 4:7.

_____

_____

_____

4. Now turn to Psalm 103:13. Even though we're made of clay, how does God relate to those who love Him?

_____

_____

_____

5. According to Isaiah 42:3, how would God treat marred clay?

_____

_____

_____

6. Though God created us from humble beginnings, in Psalm 139:13–16 (NIV) the psalmist claims we are "fearfully and wonderfully made." Rephrase these verses below using pottery-making terms. For example, instead of "My *frame* was not hidden from you," you could write, "My *clay* was not hidden from You."

_____

_____

_____

7. How do you feel about being created from humble beginnings?

_____

_____

_____

8. In what ways do you feel "wonderfully made"?

_____

_____

_____

Though we've emerged from humble beginnings, the Potter sees our raw potential for something more finished. He wraps His hands around our clay, delighted to create an intimate, individual relationship with each of us.

A Potter's Work
FORM MORE THAN FUNCTION

[A] beautiful work of art … sits in my upstairs bedroom, the kind
that beckons attention, evokes emotion, and lingers in the mind.
It is an exquisite piece of pottery that woos and teases passersby.
Half vase because of its small pedestal and half pot due to its wide
girth and mouth, this creation embodies the word "unique."

A narrow-eyed pragmatist might examine this creation and question,
"What good is it? It doesn't do anything." And yes, I could fill the pot
with pinecones and tennis balls or jewelry or whatever—just to assign
it something to do—but that would detract from its intrinsic beauty. All
things considered, I value the pottery's form more than its function.

This is how God feels about us. We are his beautiful and thoughtful
creation. Like one-of-a-kind pottery, above all he treasures our
innate worth. We are immensely significant, and our value does not
depend on anything we do, think, say, feel, earn, inherit, or look like.
It is because we exist as God's creation. Finis. Nothing more.[1]
—*Judith Couchman,* Designing a Woman's Life

About Your Value

1. How do you usually value yourself? In other words, how do you determine your self-worth?

_____

_____

_____

2. Why do we often value function more than form?

_____

_____

_____

3. How could you begin to value your form more than your function?

_____

_____

_____

Exploring the Clay
A TIMELINE VIEW OF YOU

To fully grasp the benefits of spiritual transformation, it's vital to explore the content of your clay—the beginnings and the lifetime that's formed you. The following exercises will aid this exploration and lay a foundation for the inner journey ahead. This kind of discovery takes time, so you might want to break it into several short explorations instead of an elongated one. Exploring your clay means slowing down, reflecting on the past, and pondering its meanings.

1. **Begin exploring your clay by reading the preceding excerpt ("Form More Than Function") and answering the questions.**

2. **Look back on your life from birth until the present. What people, places, experiences, and spiritual encounters influenced you? To answer these questions, use Worksheets 7–10—"A Closer Look at Your Clay"—on pages 105–108. They'll help you thoughtfully map out your life—the joys and the pains of your journey so far. Keep your eyes peeled for God's imprint on your clay and how He has shaped you and your path.**

This session likely stirred additional thoughts about the clay of your heritage, your past, and your uniqueness. To capture these feelings, jot them down in a journal or on blank pages in this workbook. They could help you prepare for evaluating, appreciating, and in some cases, letting go of the past.

✏ Soul Impressions
LOOKING AT YOUR IMPRINTS

Now think about the questions and timelines you've completed. Certain joys, pains, themes, and patterns have probably emerged. Use the following questions to pinpoint the recurring imprints in your clay and your feelings about them.

1. For what people, places, and experiences are you grateful? Why?

_____

_____

_____

2. What people, places, and experiences caused you pain? Why?

_____

_____

_____

3. For what part of your heritage, abilities, and personality are you grateful? Why?

_____

_____

_____

4. What part of your heritage, abilities, and personality would you rather not own? Why?

_____

_____

_____

5. What themes and/or patterns seem to thread throughout your life? How have they helped or hindered you?

_____

_____

_____

6. How do you perceive God's involvement in your life until now?

_____

_____

_____

If these pages can't contain your soul's outpouring—and for many of us, they aren't enough—consider writing on additional loose-leaf pages or in your own journal. Use these exercises and questions to stimulate your thinking, but don't let them limit your process.

On the Wheel
MIXED, MALLEABLE, AND MOLDED

It's joyous and painful, rewarding and unsettling, to look at our clay's shape. We all possess much to be grateful for and yet we all harbor pain we'd like to forget. God wants to mix and mold our past and present, regrets and rewards, into a beautiful vessel.

1. What aspects of your past and current shape could assist the Potter's work in your life?

_____

_____

_____

2. What aspects of your past and current shape might be inclined to resist the Potter's work?

_____

_____

_____

All of our stories about the past converge in the present. Where we've traveled influences our response to the Potter's work today and the shape of things to come. Consequently, in the formation stage—observing the clay and its components—certain acts prove crucial. They determine whether we assist or resist God's work in our lives. It is crucial to:

• Name the past, understanding its issues and influences on us.

• Forgive people and circumstances that wounded us.

• Search the past for its meaning and usefulness to us today.

• Live in gratitude for the blessings of each day.

Malleable, enduring clay yields to the Potter's tender hands. We practice this yielding by embracing these soul-searching actions. At the same time, these actions depend on choice. We can choose whether or not to step forward onto the Potter's wheel.

3. Name your past. Give it a title or catchphrase that describes it. Or use a song or movie title. Then write a few sentences that encapsulate the past's influence on your formation.

_____

_____

_____

4. Who do you need to forgive? Create a list and note how you could accomplish this for each person. You'll be able to forgive some people right away. Others will require an extended process. Ask God to turn these initial thoughts into a path of forgiveness.

_____

_____

_____

5. As best you can discern now, what is the meaning of your past? How can it prove useful to you today?

_____

_____

_____

6. For what are you grateful today? Ask yourself this every day as the Potter's hands ready you for reformation.

_____

_____

_____

Our response to the past—our malleability and forgiving spirit—plays a crucial part in how our clay reforms in the future. Looking at your clay today will reap rewards later.

Prayers to the Potter
GETTING TO KNOW YOU AND ME

Simply put, spiritual transformation involves getting to know the Divine Potter as well as ourselves. We grow into who God created us to be rather than who everyone else thinks we should be. When we know ourselves, we better understand God. When we know God, we better understand ourselves. So knowing God and knowing ourselves are not mutually exclusive. They form a Potter-and-clay bond that shapes and releases the true identity within us.

Read the following prayers from two well-known theologians. Then write your own prayer to the Potter about knowing yourself and knowing God.

Grant, Lord, that I may know myself that I may know thee.

—Saint Augustine

And now Lord, with your help, I shall become myself.

—Søren Kierkegaard

My Prayer to the Potter

_____

_____

_____

_____

_____

_____

_____

_____

Notes for the Journey
KNOWING YOURSELF, KNOWING GOD

Self-acceptance always precedes genuine self-
surrender and self-transformation.
—David Benner

There is no deep knowing of God without a deep knowing of self
and no deep knowing of self without a deep knowing of God.
—John Calvin

There is always one thing to be grateful for—that
one is one's self and not somebody else.
—Emily Dickinson

A humble self-knowledge is a surer way to God
than a search after deep learning.
—Thomas à Kempis

Apart from Christ we know neither what life nor death is; we
do not know what God is nor what we ourselves are.
—Blaise Pascal

Without self-love there can be no other self.
—Walter Trobisch

Worksheet Seven
A CLOSER LOOK AT YOUR CLAY:
THE PEOPLE WHO INFLUENCED YOU

Name your influencers. This is the first of four timelines to examine your clay. On this page place an X on the timeline for each person who significantly influenced you, positively or negatively. Write a name above each X and a few words about that person's influence.

How do you feel about these people's influences in your life? You might want to jot that down too or write more about them in a journal.

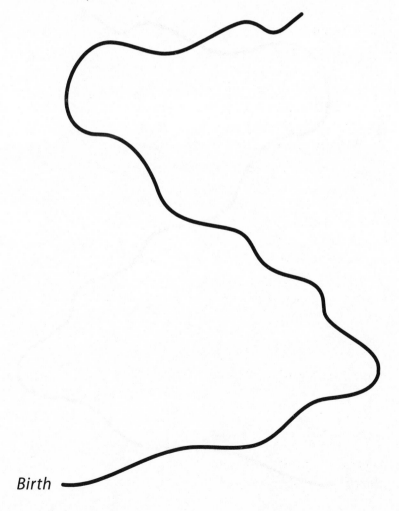

Birth

Worksheet Eight
A CLOSER LOOK AT YOUR CLAY:
THE PLACES THAT SHAPED YOU

Name your influencers. This is the second of four timelines to examine your clay. On this page place an X on the timeline for each place that significantly shaped you, positively or negatively. Write a name above each X and a few words about that place's influence.

How do you feel about these places' influences in your life? You might want to jot that down too or write more about them in a journal.

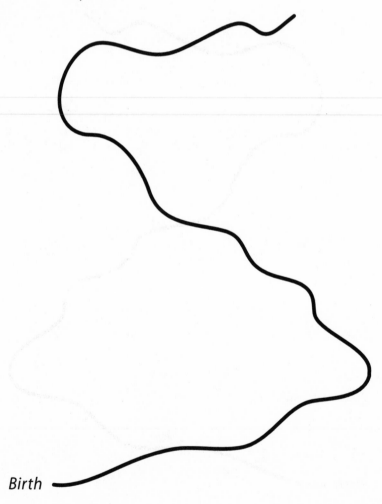

Birth

Worksheet Nine
A CLOSER LOOK AT YOUR CLAY:
THE EXPERIENCES THAT MOLDED YOU

Name your influencers. This is the third of four timelines to examine your clay. On this page place an X on the timeline for each experience that significantly molded you, either positively or negatively. Write a name above each X and a few words about that experience's influence.

How do you feel about these experiences' influences in your life? You might want to jot that down too or write more about them in a journal.

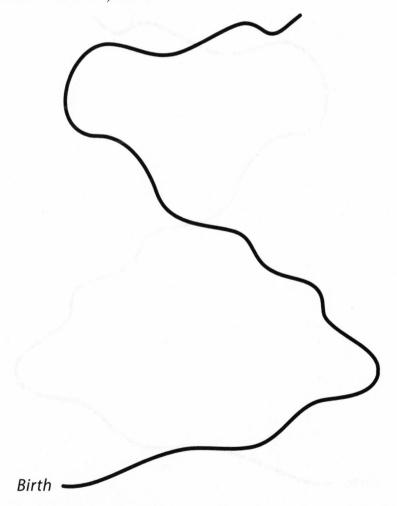

Birth

Worksheet Ten
A CLOSER LOOK AT YOUR CLAY:
THE GOD WHO CREATED YOU

Name your influencers. This is the last of four timelines to examine your clay. On this page place an X on the timeline for each encounter with God that significantly shaped your understanding of Him, yourself, or others. Write an identifying title above each X and a few words about its influence on you.

How do you feel about these spiritual encounters' influences in your life? You might want to jot that down too, or write more about them in a journal.

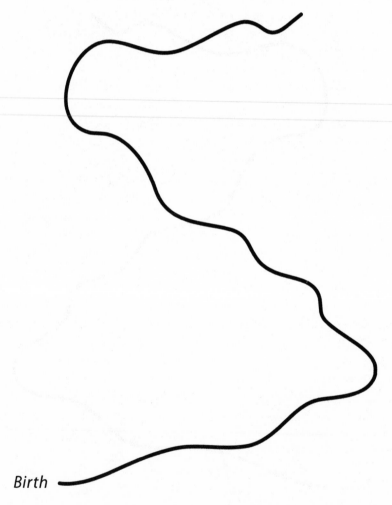

Birth

The Need to Reform

Letting the Potter reclaim your failures and disappointments

Difficulty and failure can pummel us into marred clay. But the
Potter doesn't discard us. Instead, He reclaims the clay, wasting
nothing, with an eye for its eventual beauty and usefulness.

The Need to Reform

A [person] who fails well is greater than one who succeeds badly.
—*Thomas Merton*

When Jeremiah visited the potter's house, he observed a remarkable aspect of the potter's work. He explained, "Whenever the pot the potter was working on turned out badly, as sometimes happens when you are working with clay, the potter would simply start over and use the same clay to make another pot" (Jer. 18:4). He didn't discard the marred clay. He reclaimed it. He envisioned another way to shape it.

Marred clay is imperfect; something failed in the formation process. Like the clay, our lives can turn out different than expected, possibly including a mistake, a tragedy, a dashed dream, a sinful choice, or a broken relationship. If we live long enough, we all experience pain and marring. Even Jesus didn't escape deep sorrow. Jesus was called "a man of sorrows … familiar with suffering" (Isa. 53:3 NIV). No human being escapes the challenges of failure and disappointment.

Jeremiah's encounter with the potter offers valuable insights to our failures. When our clay is marred by sin, mistakes, and difficulties, God doesn't reject us. In fact, the Potter expects flaws to surface while making a vessel. We fall apart, but no failure is so big it can't be reformed into something unique and valuable. The Potter uses the same clay. There is no refuse or throwaway parts. All of the clay—the blemishes, fractures, and failures—belong to the transformed pot.

The Potter envisions the clay and wheel from a perspective that nobody else does. So the clay needs to stay on the wheel, trust the process, and allow the strong and loving hands to work. As the wheel spins faster, the motion provides the necessary friction to change the formation. His hands surround the pot and apply enough pressure to create the shape. If the clay wobbles off center, as happens with pots and people, the Potter reforms it. If it collapses, He carefully reshapes it.

In this session, consider how God works when life disintegrates, what can be learned in the process, and the hope that's ahead for your marred clay.

RECLAIMING THE CLAY

All pottery processes create a certain amount
of waste clay—the trimmings and scraps
in the splash tray of the wheel, small coils
that have become too stiff to be workable,
or the off cuts from leather-hard slabs that
have been put aside and allowed to dry
out. Until it is fired, however, all clay can be
reclaimed to a working condition. Contrary to
expectations, clay improves with age, and if
left in a soft condition, increases its plasticity.[1]

—*Steve Mattison,* The Complete Potter

🖤 The Potter's Heart
BROKEN HEARTS, REFORMED LIVES

When we've been through a "marring time," it's comforting to know we're not alone. The Bible contains examples of sinful and broken people whom God redeems, reforming the shape of their lives. Their stories are in the Scriptures for our solace, instruction, and encouragement. The following questions focus on a few ordinary people who reached for God's mercy, expressed through Jesus Christ, in times of need.

1. The bleeding woman in Matthew 9:19–22 was considered unclean, but she approached Jesus anyway. How did He respond to her? Write down His specific words to her.

_____

_____

_____

2. In Luke 18:35–42, a blind beggar cried out to Jesus. How did the Lord respond to this man?

_____

_____

_____

3. What was similar about the way the bleeding woman and the blind man approached Jesus?

_____

_____

_____

4. In Luke 19:1–9, how did Jesus treat the tax collector?

_____

_____

_____

5. From these biblical examples, what can you learn about approaching God in your time
   of need?

_____

_____

_____

When we are reformed, a myriad of feelings emerge within us: pain, distress, bewilderment, frustration. In the second book of Corinthians, Paul helped Christians explore their feelings about difficulty and being reformed. We can glean wisdom from his insights.

6. Read 2 Corinthians 7:9. Paul describes a time of distress that upset the Christians at
   Corinth: "You were jarred into turning things around. You let the distress bring you to
   God, not drive you from him. The result was all gain, no loss." How did distress affect
   these Corinthians? Why would they respond this way?

_____

_____

_____

7. How would turning to God have caused "all gain, no loss"?

_____

_____

_____

8. Paul continues to help the Corinthians explore this significant experience. In verse 10 he writes, "Distress that drives us to God does that. It turns us around. It gets us back in the way of salvation. We never regret that kind of pain. But those who let distress drive them away from God are full of regrets, and end up on a deathbed of regrets." What options does Paul give about how people respond to pain, distress, and times of reformation?

_____

_____

_____

9. In verse 10, Paul says, "We never regret that kind of pain." What do you think he means? Do you agree?

_____

_____

_____

10. In verses 11–12, Paul also says there is another benefit to difficult times: "And now, isn't it wonderful all the ways in which this distress has goaded you closer to God? You're more alive, more concerned, more sensitive, more reverent, more human, more passionate, and more responsible. Looked at from any angle, you've come out of this with purity of heart." Choose two of the words Paul uses and evaluate your own experience with what Paul describes. Which quality do you most need? Which quality do you most want? Which one causes you to pause and think more deeply about who you could become?

_____

_____

_____

At some point you can further explore the Bible, learning how God redeemed additional people and difficulties. But for now, as you progress through this session, keep in mind the biblical people and assurances you've just read.

A Potter's Work
THE MESSY ART OF TRANSFORMATION

Life isn't easy. Neither is spiritual transformation. Like clay whirling on a potter's wheel, it's messy. Dirty water. Lumpy clay. Drippy hands. Sometimes the clay slumps, and the potter catches and reshapes it. Sometimes shaping the vessel takes more time than imagined. The Potter demonstrates that spiritual transformation isn't clean or clear cut. Nor is the reforming process linear or sequential in order. It's more of an art form than an exact science. We can't predict or control everything that will happen.

In contrast, we want how-to steps that manage our lives and lead us neatly out of our troubles. But when we get fired, the doctor diagnoses cancer, a child uses drugs, a marriage fails, or we're stuck in an addiction, lists and steps can fail us and our faith. Consequently, we need to accept that spiritual transformation is circular, unpredictable, and sometimes feels like we're falling back instead of stepping forward. It's messy, but God the Potter holds us.

No potter works with clean hands. He touches the messy clay, working out its impurities and reforming its shape. It is the same way when God works in us. We bring a messy life—our impure clay—to the transformation process. The Potter works in the mess with soiled hands oozing with wet, soft clay. Without His mud-spattered hands, our trouble could turn into hopelessness.

Could it be that the Potter thrives on the chaos of the whirling wheel? Could it be that He loves messes? The Potter places His hands on slumping clay and turns it into a masterpiece. We bring the trouble. The Potter works the transformation.

About Your Mess

1. What mess in your life needs God's handiwork?

_____

_____

_____

2. How would you describe this mess right now?

_____

_____

_____

3. Can you observe God working in this mess? If not, why? If so, how?

_____

_____

_____

Exploring Your Clay
A LOOK AT YOUR LIFE NOW

In the previous sessions you explored your past: your feelings about the hands in your life; the shape of who you are; the people, places, and events that formed you. Hopefully you've seen God at work in your life so far. When you see God's goodness in the past, you can hope for His mercy in the present, especially if you're in a time of difficulty.

Now think about your life. What feels marred or broken? What needs reforming by the Potter's tender hands? These next exercises will help you sort through needs and thoughts.

1. **If you haven't already, read "The Messy Art of Transformation" on page 118 and answer the questions.**

2. **We all have messes, problems, and wounds in our lives. We've caused pain. We've been wounded by others. However these challenges occur, it helps to realistically look at the situation, assessing its impact on you and others. This is necessary before stepping toward change. If you feel ready, Worksheet 11—"Mapping Out Your Life"—on page 127 can assist in sorting out a current challenge in your life. As you complete the worksheet, remember God's hovering hands, ready to lovingly transform you and your difficulties. If you don't feel ready for this exercise, move on to the next section.**

When life turns out badly, we yearn for another chance. In the next section, you can express that desire to God. Like many of God's followers in the Bible, pour out your heart to Him, asking for His mercy, strength, and redemption.

Soul Impressions
FEELING THE PRESSURE

Once we recognize the scope of a difficulty, we can't escape feelings about it. Just as it's helpful to examine the challenge, it's good to explore our opinions and hopes about it. Jesus expressed His pain to God, and so can we. This is a step toward healing. The Potter's hands can sensitively handle our responses to the pressure.

1. On a scale of 1 to 10, with 1 as "not intense" and 10 as "intense," rate the following aspects regarding the "messy" situation you described in "A Potter's Work," question 1.

   _____ The pain I feel about this problem

   _____ The hope I harbor that God will redeem these circumstances

   _____ The desperation I feel about needing to change myself

   _____ The concern I have for other people this problem has affected

   _____ The desire I have for other people in this situation to change

2. Summarize how you feel about this problem and your need for God's reforming touch and redemption.

   _____

   _____

   _____

3. In the midst of this challenge, how would you like God to reform you?

   _____

   _____

   _____

4. How do you need God's daily assistance and redemption?

_____

_____

_____

🖊 On the Wheel
A SOUL ADVOCATE

People respond to pain and difficulty in various ways. Some flee. Others fight. Some turn inward. Others talk and talk. However you respond, you need companionship during this time—a person or group who will walk with you through the reforming process.

1. We all develop coping mechanisms in response to difficulty, and many of them try to avoid engaging in the problem. How do you usually respond to pain? Check all the descriptions that apply.

   _____ I run away from it.

   _____ I try to deny its existence.

   _____ I fight the problem.

   _____ I try to fix the problem myself.

   _____ I blame other people.

   _____ I feel sorry for myself.

   _____ I take responsibility for my part.

   _____ I ask God for help and wait for Him.

   _____ I look for another person to understand me.

   _____ Other(s) _____

2. When you experience the reforming process, it's comforting to have someone to confide in, a person who loves and believes in you. You need a soulful advocate in your life. Turn to Worksheet 12—"A Soulful Advocate"—on page 129 to consider the kind of person who would effectively walk with you through this time.

When we consider companionship for the reforming process, keep in mind that different personalities need different kinds of soulful advocacy. Introverts tend to seek out one or two friends. Extroverts might need a group setting. Either way, it's important to have at least one person who will support, encourage, and love you no matter what. Ask God for that person in your life.

Prayers to the Potter
ENTERING THE HOPEFUL SILENCE

After the prophet Jeremiah describes the trouble, the feeling of utter lostness, and the taste of ashes in his life, he remembers one thing: He can hope in God (Lam. 3:19–21). Read the passage below to find out what he recommends to people who have been marred and broken by life.

> *God proves to be good to the man who passionately waits, to the woman who diligently seeks.*
>
> *It is a good thing to quietly hope, quietly hope for help from God....*
>
> *When life is heavy and hard to take, go off by yourself. Enter the silence.*
>
> *Bow in prayer. Don't ask questions; wait for hope to appear.*
>
> *Don't run from trouble. Take it full [force]. The worst is never the worst.*
>
> *Why? Because the Master won't ever walk out and fail to return.*
>
> *If he works severely, he also works tenderly. His stockpiles of loyal love are immense. (Lam. 3:25–26, 28–32)*

Jeremiah urges us to enter the silence and wait for God's hope and help. While we wait, we don't need to utter words. We can sit in silent prayer. In his book, *Silence on Fire,* William Shannon describes this wordless prayer. He writes, "Wordless prayer is humble, simple, lovely prayer in which we experience our total dependence on God and our awareness that we are in God. Wordless prayer is not an effort to 'get anywhere,' for we are already in God's presence."[2]

Sometime this week, carve out time to sit in solitude, in God's presence, in silent prayer. Begin by telling the Lord that you're waiting in silence for His hope and love. Then wait in quiet expectation until you're at peace. You might discover this as a helpful weekly or daily practice, especially when passing through difficulty.

Notes for the Journey
THOUGHTS ON CHANGING YOUR LIFE

Often, in order to stay alive, we have to "unmake" a living in order
to get back to living the life we wanted for ourselves.
—David Whyte

God's love does not allow us to remain as we are. It is more than
acceptance. It works and forms, it carves out the image which God
has intended. This is a lifelong process and sometimes a painful one.
Since growth is connected with pain, God says I accept you as you
are, but now the work of love begins. I need your cooperation.
—Walter Trobisch

Here, in this "place," God is at work, bending, breaking, molding, doing
just as he chooses. Why he is doing it, we do not know; he is doing it for
one purpose only—that he is able to say, "This is my man, my woman."
—Oswald Chambers

God loves you the way you are, but he loves you
too much to let you stay like this.
—Bumper sticker

Worksheet Eleven
MAPPING OUT YOUR LIFE

Looking at your life. Sometimes when you're in difficulty it's hard to believe the mess you're in has even occurred. Thinking about the issue long enough to grasp how it has affected you and others can be painful. But part of allowing the Potter to mercifully reform your life is "owning" the situation, that is coming out of denial and facing the problem.

Creating a cluster map can help. It's a simple way to look at your life and the marring in your clay, whether or not you caused the problem. You can also use this method for creating action steps during a time of reformation.

The diagram below shows how a problem or goal can be mapped, looking at each person or aspect of life that's affected, exploring feelings, and compounding events. Turn to the back of this worksheet for directions and a diagram you can use. Or, if you prefer, use a blank sheet of paper and draw your own map.

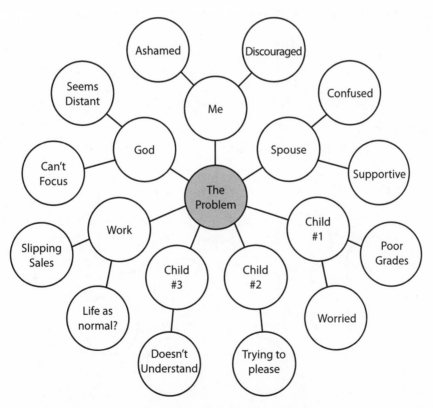

Worksheet Eleven
MAPPING OUT YOUR LIFE

Making your map. Use the diagram below or your own sheet of paper to map out the problem that needs the Potter's reforming hands.

1. **In the center circle, write the problem.**

2. **In the circles radiating around it, fill in the people or situations that have been affected by the problem. Add circles if necessary.**

3. **For each of these people or situations, you can draw more lines and circles to indicate how the problem has affected them. See the example on the other side.**

4. **Continue drawing lines and circles and filling in the circles. Explore the problem as far as it's affected people and situations in your life. Don't forget to identify good aspects and responses among the stresses.**

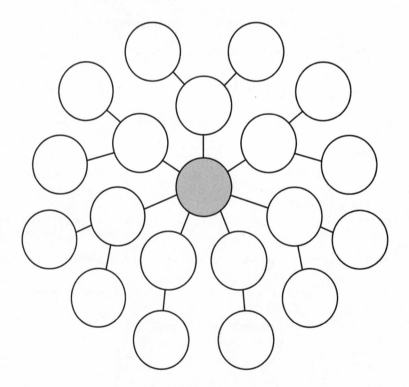

Worksheet Twelve
A SOULFUL ADVOCATE

Someone who believes in you. When you pass through the reforming process, it's comforting to have someone to confide in, a person who loves and believes in you. You need a soul advocate in your life. The word *advocate* means "one called to another." A soulful advocate might be a friend, parent, sibling, teacher, mentor, spiritual director, or even a group.

In his book *Leap Over a Wall*, Eugene Peterson describes the kind of person we're longing to come alongside us and walk, hand in hand, through our difficulties and movement toward change. Read the following excerpt and ponder the questions below. They will help you pinpoint a soul advocate for your spiritual transformation.

> *Each of us has contact with hundreds of people who never look beyond our surface appearance. We have dealings with hundreds of people who the moment they set eyes on us begin calculating what use we can be to them, what they can get out of us. We meet hundreds of people who take one look at us, make a snap judgment, and then slot us into a category so that they won't have to deal with us as persons. They treat us as something less than we are; and if we're in constant association with them, we become less. And then someone enters into our life who isn't looking for someone to use, is leisurely enough to find out what's really going on in us, is secure enough not to exploit our weaknesses or attack our strengths, recognizes our inner life and understands the difficulty of living out our inner convictions, confirms what is deepest within us. A friend.*[3]

1. Do you have a soul advocate in your life now? If so, describe this person. If not, go to question 3.

   _____

   _____

   _____

2. Do you feel your current soulful advocate is suited to help you through the spiritual transformation process? If so, explain. If not, answer question 3.

_____

_____

_____

3. What characteristics do you need in a soulful advocate, particularly with the problems and situations in your life now? Why?

_____

_____

_____

The Heart of Transformation

Saying yes to the Potter and His change process

Real change emerges from the heart, by the touch of the Holy
Spirit. The Potter tends to our brokenness and begins the process
of transformation. But we must say yes to His work.

The Heart of Transformation

Every morning, I must say again to myself, today I start.
—Anthony of the Desert, second-century church father

A friend recently confessed in a small group, "I need to be transformed because I know what it is like to *not* be transformed." This friend's simple statement combined his need, confession, and desire to change.

We can all relate. Who of us would be happy to stay as we are for the rest of our lives? As faith and life converge, we desire something more. We are not satisfied to remain the same. The human soul reaches, strives, and yearns to become something different, something more like we're intended to be: the image-bearers of God. We long for deep, inner transformation.

The word *transformation* is a synonym to the Greek word *metamorphosis*. *Meta* means "change" and *morphe* means "form." We recognize the process of metamorphosis—a changed form—when the caterpillar spins its cocoon and emerges as a butterfly. We experience this metamorphosis as God the Potter works in us. According to Romans 13:12, "God is putting the finishing touches on the salvation work he began when we first believed." When we become new in Christ, He invites us on a lifelong journey of spiritual transformation.

Unfortunately, we often settle for pseudotransformation. This is a poser type of existence. It's pretending to change without authentic, internal adjustments. It's trying to change through methods that don't produce lasting results. Pseudotransformation is not the deep, soul-satisfying experience that Jesus offers. He calls the men and women who follow Him to a drastic lifestyle, relationship, and attitude change. Jesus is not interested in pseudotransformation. He calls for new birth, dying to self, loving our enemies, valuing His kingdom, and renouncing anything that competes for His place in our lives. He wants us to change from the heart.

But we can't change—we can't spiritually transform—by ourselves. Only the Potter can accomplish heartfelt change. In this session, consider the nature of transformation, the Potter's role, and how change can begin in your life.

"One of the great qualities of clay is that it never needs to be wasted, and until it is fired it can be reprocessed over and over again. Scrapings and pieces cut away from a pot in the making, and even unsuccessful pots, can be reclaimed and made back into a workable body. Different clays can be reclaimed in the same bucket to make a mixed body…. It is important to test the mixed clay before starting a piece of work, however, because it could behave unexpectedly in both handling and firing."[1]

–*Jacqui Atkin,* Handbuilt Pottery Techniques Revealed

♥ The Potter's Heart
ON THE ROAD TO TRANSFORMATION

When we need to change, we often search for advice, books, and programs to alleviate the problem. Though these can be helpful, as Christians it's crucial to remember that spiritual transformation flows from God, not from tips, techniques, and our best efforts. We need the Potter's touch. But we approach the Potter and spiritual transformation in varying ways. The Bible contains many stories of people's encounters with God and their resulting spiritual transformation. In this section, look at how Jesus encountered seekers and how He changed their lives.

1. According to 2 Corinthians 3:18, what is the purpose of spiritual transformation?

_____

_____

_____

2. Looking at the same verse, who creates this transformation?

_____

_____

_____

3. Read Luke 24:13–35. Imagine the two followers of Christ talking to one another on the road to Emmaus. How might they feel? What might they be saying?

_____

_____

_____

4. When Jesus joins the men, what questions does He ask them? (See verses 17 and 19.) What do these questions accomplish?

_____

_____

_____

5. In verses 25–26, how does Jesus use Scripture?

_____

_____

_____

6. After the men talk with Jesus and engage in the Scriptures, what happens inside them? Note what happens in verse 31 and what they say in verse 32.

_____

_____

_____

7. According to verses 33–35, the men don't keep this moment to themselves. What happens? Why do you think they do this?

_____

_____

_____

Change and transformation are what God does in us. Deep change is God's work, not ours. We do not have to remain the same. This is good news for us as we live out our lives—sometimes spinning on the wheel, sometimes waiting, sometimes not always aware of what is really happening in us.

A Potter's Work
THE GRACE OF SURRENDER

"Come to me." When the circumstances of life are beyond our ability to bear them, when there seems to be no way for things to work out, when the rapids hit and the boat threatens to capsize at any moment, when a sudden change in life plans cancels our dreams and reroutes the future, Jesus stands before us, and with his arms open wide, extends this incredible invitation. Surrendering our burdens at his feet and placing each heavy parcel before the cross, we can choose to close our ears to competing commands and confusing directions, and listen for God's voice alone....

Through surrender, bowing before God's mighty throne, laying each struggle before our Father in heaven, casting out all grief and heartache, giving up to Jesus every source of suffering and sin—we participate, with Christ, in his kingdom's victories. We cannot do it on our own. Heeding the Lord's command to surrender, we are continually surprised that, somehow, in a way beyond our comprehension, he triumphs through us.

Take heart, then. Pray for the grace of surrender. Receive all the peace and love Jesus freely offers. He is waiting. His arms are open.[2]
—*Debra Evans,* Women of Character

About Your Invitation

1. What challenge or area of your life might God be asking you to surrender to Him?

_____

_____

_____

2. If you surrender, what would this look like in your life?

_____

_____

_____

3. How might surrender affect your process of spiritual transformation?

_____

_____

_____

Exploring Your Clay
TRYING HARD TO CHANGE

We all have stories about trying to change—losing weight, getting past anger, handling our money better, stopping addictive behavior. We all have times when our efforts failed. In this section, look at your efforts to change—the times you succeeded at changing and the times you didn't—and think about what factors contributed to this.

1. Think of a time when you tried to change and it didn't work. Describe it below.

_____

2. What contributed to your failure to change?

_____

3. How did you feel about this inability to change?

_____

4. Think of another time when you tried to change and you were successful. Describe it below.

_____

5. What contributed to your ability to change?

_____

_____

_____

6. Read the excerpt that appears just before this section and answer the questions.

It's difficult to implement lasting change, and it's helpful to remember the principles that assisted our change in the past. On the other hand, we can also remember why certain efforts to change haven't lasted. In some cases, we may have mistaken real spiritual transformation for a fake transformation.

Soul Impressions
WHAT IS AUTHENTIC AND WHAT IS NOT?

What is authentic spiritual transformation? It begins with surrender to the Potter. But other factors, attitudes, and relationships contribute to our ability to really change. Take time to contrast the difference between authentic and pseudotransformation and the roles they've played in your life.

Turn to Worksheet 13—"What Is Authentic Transformation?"—on page 147. Explore the chart that describes authentic transformation versus pseudotransformation. To clarify the difference between the two, answer the questions at the end of the chart.

1. What characteristics of authentic transformation do you already have in your life? You may need to consult the chart on page 147 again.

   _____

   _____

   _____

2. What elements of authentic transformation would you like to develop in your life?

   _____

   _____

   _____

3. Are there any parts of authentic transformation that you resist, or don't understand? Explain.

   _____

   _____

   _____

4. What elements of pseudotransformation exist in your life?

_____

_____

_____

5. What initial thoughts do you have about changing these pseudo elements of transformation into authentic ones?

_____

_____

_____

When we're ready for real change—authentic spiritual transformation—we can say yes to the Potter's work. We might be surprised, though, to learn that as much as we crave change, we can also harbor resistance toward it.

On the Wheel
SAYING YES TO REAL CHANGE

Though the Potter is the source of real change, it's our decision to cooperate with how He brings about spiritual transformation.

1. **Read the excerpt on page 145 and answer the questions. Explore your own resistance to trouble and transformation.**

2. **Turn to Worksheet 14—"Getting to Yes"—on page 149. Use it to evaluate your attitude toward spiritual transformation. How much do you want it? What do you fear or resist about it? Are you ready to say yes to real change?**

If you're holding back from the Potter's wheel, ask God to help you be ready. Remember: "A bruised reed he will not break, and a smoldering wick he will not snuff out" (Isa. 42:3 NIV). It is not God's intention to destroy, but to heal and bring the change you need. Tender hands hover over you, lovingly reshaping your life as they work out the changes you need.

Prayers to the Potter
MELT MY RESISTANCE, LORD

When we look at our need for transformation, we're prone to resist. It sounds unfamiliar and uncomfortable. It seems easier to stick with what we know. But challenges in our lives usually don't improve if we ignore them. If you're feeling resistant, this prayer by Robert Mulholland Jr., could help melt you into God's transforming love.

> *God … by your grace soften my hardness and rigidity; help me to become*
> *pliable in your hands. Even as I read this, may there be a melting of my innate*
> *resistance to your transforming love. Amen.*[3]

This week, observe the ways you might be resisting God's hands at work in your life. When you recognize your resistance, verbally or silently say this prayer to Him.

Notes for the Journey
REBELLION AS A FIRST STEP

Rebellion! That is the usual reaction [to trouble], and no one needs to be
ashamed of feeling rebellious when fate strikes him. Most people hide it, but
the first reaction, the normal reaction in the eyes of a psychologist or
a doctor, is revolt. Open your Bible, and you will see that the greatest
believers were rebels—Isaiah, Jeremiah, and all the rest. There were
even movements of rebellion in Jesus himself. So do not be ashamed
of rebellion. It is normal. It is necessary to be able to pass through
this zone of indignation in order to reach true acceptance, not by
an effort of the will, but with the present help of the Spirit.

The purpose of life is not the absence of suffering, but that the suffering
should bear fruit. Jesus warned his followers that they would experience
tribulation and persecution. And St. Francis said, "The good that I wait for is
so great that all pain is joy to me." That is the triumph of the Spirit and of faith
that can transform suffering into the joy of knowing God more intimately....

Our aim is to help humanity look at things no longer only in their
technological, external, inhuman aspect, but also to see what is
at stake on the human level, in the life of every person. This is the
struggle of faith that can find meaning even in suffering, in failure
and amputation, and win through to intimacy with the Savior.[4]
—*Paul Tournier,* A Listening Ear

About Your Resistance

1. What is your first reaction to trouble?

_____

_____

_____

2. When do you usually feel rebellious?

_____

_____

_____

3. How can rebellion be used for good in your spiritual transformation process?

_____

_____

_____

Worksheet Thirteen
WHAT IS AUTHENTIC TRANSFORMATION?

Two kinds of change. We can experience two types of transformation: a pseudotransformation that only touches the surface of our personalities, or authentic transformation that affects the soul and activates real change. Explore the following chart, contrasting the differences between the two types of transformation and look up the scriptures. Then answer the questions that follow.[5]

Authentic Transformation	*Pseudotransformation*
What our hearts are reaching for—our new frontier.	**Where we've been before—previously explored territory.**
Faces the truth. (Romans 7:15-25; John 8:31-32)	Perpetuates a lie and excuses behavior. "I don't have a problem." Or, "Everyone does this."
Realizes the importance of the heart. (I Samuel 16:7; Proverbs 4:23)	Lives on the surface and from the surface.
Embraces a process. (Jeremiah 18:1-6; Ephesians 4:13-15)	Frantically looks for answers in steps, logic, and laws. Watches the clock.
Requires surrender and humility. *"I can't do it. God, please help me."* (Matthew 26:39; James 4:10; 1 Peter 5:6)	Insists on self-help and self-reliance for change.
Changes from the inside out. (Matthew 23:25; Mark 7:18-23)	Outside, external changes.
Collaborative and cooperative. (Philippians 2:12; there are 54 "one another" statements in the New Testament)	Competitive and judgmental. Comparing ourselves to others and their progress versus our own.
Individually designed process. (Psalm 139:13-15)	Cookie-cutter program. Everyone must follow the same path.
Spirit-driven process. (John 14:26-27; John 16:13-15)	Human-driven process.
Admits brokenness. (2 Corinthians 4:7-12)	Portrays a polished façade.
Values community. (Ecclesiastes 4:9-12; Matthew 18:19-20)	Desperado or Lone-Ranger mentality.

1. In one sentence, summarize the nature of pseudotransformation.

_____

_____

_____

2. In one sentence, summarize the nature of authentic transformation.

_____

_____

_____

3. What do you think is the key difference between pseudo and authentic transformation?

_____

_____

_____

Worksheet Fourteen
GETTING TO YES

The resistance factor. Even though we desire change, we can still resist it. The two feelings are not mutually exclusive. After the statements below, rate your current receptivity to spiritual transformation by circling the response closest to how you feel. Then complete the other side of this page too.

1. I am afraid of God making changes in my life.

☐ No ☐ A little ☐ Somewhat ☐ Yes ☐ Don't know

2. I am still uncertain what spiritual transformation will bring to my life.

☐ No ☐ A little ☐ Somewhat ☐ Yes ☐ Don't know

3. I think I can make some changes on my own, without help from others.

☐ No ☐ A little ☐ Somewhat ☐ Yes ☐ Don't know

4. I am holding back certain aspects of my life from change.

☐ No ☐ A little ☐ Somewhat ☐ Yes ☐ Don't know

5. I would like to say yes to God's work in my life, but still feel resistant.

☐ No ☐ A little ☐ Somewhat ☐ Yes ☐ Don't know

Worksheet Fourteen
GETTING TO YES

What holds you back? Use these questions to examine your resistance and assist your progress toward letting the Potter work in you. Write your answers in the space on the right side of the page.

No.

1. Where are you now?

    ↓

2. Why do you hold back?

    ↓

3. What can you do?

    ↓

4. Who will help you?

    ↓

5. How will you say yes?

    ↓

Yes.

1. _____

_____

_____

2. _____

_____

_____

3. _____

_____

_____

4. _____

_____

_____

5. _____

_____

_____

The Potter's Tools

Recognizing the things God uses to transform you

To transform our clay, the Potter uses certain tools to accomplish
His healing and creative changes. We can learn to recognize them,
appreciating their presence and power in our daily lives.

The Potter's Tools

God never hastens and he never tarries. He works his plans
out in his own way, and we either lie like clogs in his hands
or we assist him by being clay in the Potter's hands.
—*Oswald Chambers*

Artists employ tools to create their artwork. A painter selects various brushes. A wood craftsman uses saws, blades, and drills to make furniture. Even a potter uses more than bare hands to shape His creation. For example, a dampened sponge adds moisture to hardened clay. Blades cut away extraneous pieces. A brush adds unique designs. Quills leave precise impressions that add distinctiveness. A potter can also use combs, ribs, knives, brushes, and cutting wires to shape and decorate pottery.

God the Potter also uses tools to shape and reform us, pulling them from everyday life. An event could redirect our goals. A wounding might change our priorities. Scripture can guide how we relate to difficult people. A friend might point out bad habits. Children will stretch our patience. Work failures can prompt us to assess our true value. Because the Potter works with so many individuals—each with a unique personality and particular circumstances—He keeps countless tools at His disposal. The tools He uses vary from person to person.

Viewed from this perspective, Scripture tells stories about the tools God used to reshape the souls of people. Jonathan helped David when he was in danger and Naomi became a lifetime companion for Ruth. Moses walked the wilderness. Jonah changed his mind in the belly of an enormous fish. Prophets were used to warn the nation of Israel. Paul's temporary blindness helped to convert him. God uses anyone and anything to shape the souls of those He loves! Consequently, we can read these stories for comfort and guidance during our own journey of spiritual transformation.

We can also learn to recognize the tools God lovingly brings to our lives. In this session, explore a few of the tools that God uses to shape and reform us.

> "In practical terms the attraction of clay is its malleability, the fact that it faithfully records the imprint of forces brought to bear upon it and responds in the most positive way to the form-giving hand. This receptivity to being shaped, and the subsequent retention of the given shape upon drying, is known as 'plasticity.' Because of its plasticity clay can be pulled up into high thin-walled forms without tearing or subsequent slumping. It allows a shape once formed to be radically modified or indeed totally altered without collapse or disintegration and, further, it allows satellite forms such as handles, spouts, or high relief decoration to be welded on to the parent mass and to retain this positive adhesion as the clay stiffens and dries."[1]
> —*John Dickerson,* Pottery Making: A Complete Guide

♥ The Potter's Heart
TOOLS OF TRANSFORMATION

God works creatively, even mysteriously, in our lives. There's no predictable way that He brings about spiritual transformation. It looks different in every person, as unique as our individuality. However, there are some tools that He uses to change us, based on Scripture. Examine a few by reading what the Bible says about them. Remember that this isn't a complete look at all of the Potter's tools, but rather a review of some we can identify and even use ourselves.

Learning to Wait

1. Transformation occurs over time, so often we must wait. We may need to wait for changes in people, other circumstances, or ourselves. What insights about waiting do the following verses offer?

   • **Isaiah 30:18**

   _____

   _____

   _____

   • **Isaiah 40:30–31** (Some versions say "wait" and some say "hope.")

   _____

   _____

   _____

Understanding Our Wounds

2. Whatever the sources of our wounds, God can use them to spiritually transform us. This includes wounds inflicted by events, people, and circumstances beyond

our control. Or the wounds we've inflicted upon ourselves from sin, mistakes, or self-condemnation. What do these next verses reveal about our wounds?

• **Job 5:17–18**

_____

_____

_____

• **Psalm 147:3**

_____

_____

_____

• **Isaiah 53:4–5**

_____

_____

_____

Embracing the Word

3. God's Word, the Bible, teaches us general principles for living. But it can also speak to us personally, giving specific help on the path to spiritual transformation. How can Scripture help us while we're pursuing change?

• **Psalm 119:52**

_____

_____

_____

- **Psalm 119:105**

_____

_____

_____

- **2 Timothy 3:16**

_____

_____

_____

Offering Our Worship

4. Both personal and corporate worship can contribute to spiritual transformation. Worship transitions the focus from us to God. We adore Him as the Potter, appreciating His ability to comfort, heal, change, guide, and strengthen us. According to these verses, how do we worship?

- **Psalm 95:6**

_____

_____

_____

- **Psalm 100:2**

_____

_____

_____

• **Psalm 22:22**

_____

_____

_____

5. Which of the Potter's tools do you find the easiest to cooperate with? Which are the
   most difficult to cooperate with? Why?

_____

_____

_____

Each of us responds differently to the Potter's tools. For example, some people find it easy and uplifting to worship; others have to work at it. When in pain, some can't open their Bibles, and others gather comfort from the Word. Some of us fight the wounds and waiting; others flee or turn passive. The next section will help you think through your relationship to these tools.

A Potter's Work
THE PLACE OF BECOMING

Some people think of waiting as a waste of time. But something transformational happens when we learn to wait. When the caterpillar spins its cocoon, it is not a place of escape or entrapment. It becomes a sanctuary of change, a place of waiting, a place of becoming. In its dark, self-spun haven, the caterpillar enters to wait for its transforming rebirth. It will emerge into the world reformed, different. Transformation involves waiting and there's no shortcut around it.

When we are wrapped by pressure and enshrouded in obscurity, waiting can become a safe asylum to hear God and change. When we wait and are still, God comes near (Ps. 46:10). He can be heard, sensed, and experienced in a time of waiting like no other time. Jonah finally heard God when he waited in the cocoon of the fish's belly for three days. Esther fasted and waited before she approached the king. Paul stayed in Arabia for three years after his conversion. Something important happens in the waiting time—something happens when we wait that cannot happen when we are moving. When we move quickly, sometimes we allow no time for God.

Waiting at its best loses the unimportant and seizes the eternally significant. Waiting is a necessary step for spiritual maturity. The wings of butterflies and eagles grow while they wait. So do our spiritual wings. We gain strength when we wait.

About Your Waiting Time

1. What are you waiting for in your life?

_____

_____

_____

2. What is happening in you while you wait?

_____

_____

_____

3. How can you invite God closer during your waiting times?

_____

_____

_____

Exploring Your Clay
WHERE ARE YOU NOW?

We all have different ideas about, and relationships to, the transformational tools of waiting, wounds, the Word, and worship. Turn to Worksheet 15—"You and the Potter's Tools"—on page 167 and process your thinking and attitudes toward these tools.

The tools of transformation form a two-way process. God uses them, but so do we. For example, we read the Word and the Holy Spirit speaks through it. We can declare our wounds as a means for growth and hearing from God. Ask the Potter to cultivate the desire, people, and opportunities to accept and use His tools in the spiritual transformation process. They can guide, comfort, and inspire.

Soul Impressions
THE IMPORTANCE OF TALKING

In addition to the four "W" tools, there's transformational power in conversation. At any point in a life journey, but especially when we're trying to change, "talking it out" with the right person or people can make a difference.

1. **Turn to Worksheet 16—"The Power of Conversation"—on page 170 to learn how Jesus modeled conversation—and how it can empower spiritual transformation.**

2. **Now go to "The Hope of Endurance" on page 165. Answer those questions too.**

How could conversation affect the ability to endure?

_____

_____

_____

As with anything else in the change process, conversation can align with our personality and circumstantial needs. But it's important to have a safe place to unburden ourselves, clarify thinking, and gain encouragement. This also helps us to gain endurance.

On the Wheel
A TOOL TO CALL YOUR OWN

This session has covered some important transformational tools, but we don't have to tackle them all at once. That only adds stress to the change process. Instead, choose one of the tools to concentrate on, employing any of these suggestions. Add another tool as God leads, forming a natural rather than a forced process. If you choose the tool of waiting, use the "The Place of Becoming" on page 159.

1. Pray and ask God to reveal how this tool can enhance your transformation.

2. Discover more of what the Bible says about this tool.

3. Explore available material to read about this tool.

4. Engage in a meaningful conversation about this tool.

5. Begin practicing this tool in your everyday life.

As you explore the transformational tools, remember that they aren't just hard work or necessarily painful. There's also joy in waiting, wounds, the Word, worship, and conversation. Look for what's wonderful in the tools, and allow yourself to appreciate them. Even if you're in difficulty, there can be pockets of pleasure. Joy and pain often coexist.

Prayers to the Potter
SAYING THE PSALMS

When we pass through transforming times, sometimes prayer eludes us. We aren't sure what to say anymore. Enter the Psalms. They often utter what we can't. For the next four days, pray the following Old Testament psalms to God. They're focused on concepts explored in this session. Perhaps these psalms will unlock some feelings, questions, or requests that you haven't put into words yet. At the very least, soak in their comfort.

Day 1	*Day 2*	*Day 3*	*Day 4*
Waiting Psalm 130	Wounds Psalm 109:21–31	Word Psalm 119:1–16	Worship Psalm 146

Notes for the Journey
THE HOPE OF ENDURANCE

We don't want to have to endure anything painful in our lives. Diet, exercise, job loss, broken relationships, illness, and devastation are pressures we'd escape if we could. We'd rather be healed now, skinny now, comfortable now, and pain-free now! We want change without the process. We want transformation without looking awkward. To endure the agony of something that has disrupted or upset our lives is something we would rather not do. No healthy person likes suffering or pain. Enduring pain is difficult. To endure anything that is uncomfortable seems unnatural. We want to squirm, move, and escape any situation or occasion that makes us uncomfortable.

The word *endure* means "to remain under." To endure something is *to remain under* the influence. When a person endures pain, they have to remain under pain and build up a level of endurance or perseverance. An athlete who is injured has to endure practice, therapy, and persistence to move with agility. But without the persistence of the training, the exercises, and the help, there will be no easing the pain.

The image of a potter working on the clay in Jeremiah 18 teaches us a powerful truth about remaining under the hands of the masterful Potter. He sees in His mind's eye the final image. But the clay needs to endure the process. The clay must remain under the Potter's influence. As the clay is formed, reformed, and transformed, change occurs. The clay could not simply wish to be different. It yields to the hands of the Potter and remains under His touch, care, and vision.

What would the clay be if it were to escape God the Potter's hands? Clay! But when the clay yields to the process of enduring the pressure and squeeze of the Potter's hands, something fantastic happens! Purpose emerges from brokenness. Beauty exudes from the damp, cold clay. Something that seemed ruined is transformed. What happened to the clay in Jeremiah's story can happen to us. That is our hope.

About Your Endurance

1. What are your current feelings about the need to endure?

_____

_____

_____

2. When is it difficult for you to endure?

_____

_____

_____

3. Specifically, what do you imagine your reward to be if you endure during a difficult time?

_____

_____

_____

Worksheet Fifteen
YOU AND THE POTTER'S TOOLS

What's your posture toward the Potter's tools? Honestly explore your attitude and relationship toward waiting, wounds, the Word, and worship. Answer each of the questions below, as they relate to each tool.

1. What has been your attitude toward this transformation tool?

_____

_____

_____

2. What is powerful about this tool? What is beneficial?

_____

_____

_____

3. How might God be using this tool to transform you?

_____

_____

_____

4. How can you use this tool, along with receiving guidance from the Potter, as you move toward change?

_____

_____

_____

Waiting

1. _____

2. _____

3. _____

4. _____

5. _____

Wounds

1. _____

2. _____

3. _____

4. _____

5. _____

The Word

1. _____

2. _____

3. _____

4. _____

5. _____

Worship

1. _____

2. _____

3. _____

4. _____

5. _____

Worksheet Sixteen
THE POWER OF CONVERSATION

Talking it out. Conversation can be another powerful tool of transformation. Sometimes talking about a challenge points us in the direction of healing change. Read the following piece and answer the questions to think about how conversation might help you.

Jesus used conversation as a means of caring for people. He invited men and women into dialogue that changed hearts, transformed lives, and straightened ways. Through talking, listening, questioning, and exploring, they moved from self-centered misery to being kingdom-seekers.

Jesus probed with questions that riveted people's souls. He wasn't coercive or manipulative. His ordinary language crafted stories and parables that served as mirrors. On one level, the stories reflected intriguing characters and dilemmas. On another level, they reflected the lives of listeners. On the deepest level, they glimpsed the heart of God.

Jesus preferred dialogue that invited people to explore themselves and their motives. He ushered people into a deeper understanding of themselves, others, and the ways of God. Jesus was also an active listener. Through guided conversations, He helped people speak embedded spiritual realities that they couldn't articulate. He helped them find their words, their stories.

Jesus was not about crisis management, urgency, putting out fires, or driving the equivalent of a first-century ambulance. He wasn't survival-driven, but soul-driven. He recognized a person's worth and value by showing up, investing time, and initiating questions or provocative statements that helped His followers evaluate their lives, spiritual practices, relationships, and purposes. Questions like, "Does anyone here condemn you?" Statements like, "You must be born again."

A good conversation is not the giving of advice or the imparting of information.

A good conversation is:

• the invitation to explore.

• the exchange of thoughts and ideas.

• the emotional safety to say what one really means.

• the luxury of being heard and understood.

• the experience of being wanted, even by God.

• the feeling we've retrieved a part of our souls.

In our age of isolation, loneliness, and fractured communities, conversations help us find each other, our true selves, and our connection with the living God. Conversations connect us with a spiritual extended family. The loneliness we experience—called by some physicians "the disease upon which all other illnesses depend"—is soothed by connection *to God and others*.

1. What elements are helpful to you in conversation?

_____

_____

_____

2. How can you engage in conversation that supports spiritual transformation?

_____

_____

_____

3. Who could be this kind of conversationalist for you?

_____

_____

_____

The Freedom to Conform

Entering into a life that reflects the image of Christ

As the Divine Potter works on our clay, He keeps the finished product in mind. He wants us to conform to the image of His Son, Jesus Christ.

The Freedom to Conform

God allows us time to become stronger and more proficient
in our ability to walk this way, in the Spirit.

—John of the Cross

Remember how to put a jigsaw puzzle together? You pick up the puzzle box, dump out all the pieces on a table or floor, and begin. You keep an image of the finished product in mind, following the picture on top of the puzzle box. The top of the box shows what the puzzle will look like when the hundreds of pieces lock together. Without the top of the box, it would be hard to know where to begin.

> "If a teapot does not pour, or a casserole cannot survive the oven, then however good it looks, it will be useless. A pot must function well to be successful, but that function must also embrace giving pleasure to the user."[1]
>
> *—Alex McErlain,* Art of Throwing

In a similar fashion, we can keep a top-of-the-box image of the larger picture on our journey of faith. Life's jagged edges can confuse how all the pieces will fit together. So we need to keep in mind our goal: conformity to Christ's image. Throughout our Christian pilgrimage, the Divine Potter shapes, forms, presses, and reforms us to become like Jesus.

Paul states this ultimate goal in Galatians 4:19. Several Bible translations and paraphrases can clarify the meaning for us. Consider this list.

1. Until Christ is formed in you (NIV; NKJV).

2. Until Christ's life becomes visible in your lives (MSG).

3. Until Christ is completely and permanently formed (molded) within you (AB).

4. Until Christ is fully developed in your lives (NLT).

5. Until Christ may be seen living in you (CEV).

The Divine Potter uses the details of our lives to pinch here, press there, and shape us into the image of Jesus. He works to create a resemblance of Christ's character in us. However, this isn't a forced conformity. Instead, transformation loosens what binds us and sets us free to be like Christ. We are marked by His magnificent love.

In this session, explore the "top of the box" to gain a clearer perspective on the Potter's ultimate goal for our spiritual transformation.

♥ The Potter's Heart
THE IMAGE OF CHRIST

What does it mean to conform to the image of Christ? Many passages in the Bible describe Christ's actions and character and, over time, they create a revealing and important study. For now, look up the following scriptures to form a picture of the Potter's ultimate goal for your character.

1. According to these verses, how do we learn to live as individuals transformed by the Potter's tender hands?

   • **Ephesians 5:1, 8–10**

   _____

   _____

   _____

   • **1 Peter 2:21**

   _____

   _____

   _____

   • **1 John 2:6**

   _____

   _____

   _____

2. When we live by God's Spirit, as Jesus did, what qualities will we express? See Galatians 5:22–23.

_____

_____

_____

3. In verse 24, what happens to our sinful ways?

_____

_____

_____

4. Read Philippians 2:1–11. How does conformity to Christ's image affect our relationships with others?

_____

_____

_____

5. How does bearing the image of Christ affect our relationship with God?

_____

_____

_____

6. How does the attitude of Jesus differ from the current world's understanding of success?

_____

_____

_____

7. What did Jesus give up to gain this kind of attitude? See verses 6–8.

_____

_____

_____

8. According to Philippians 2:12–13, how do we gain the ability to live in a manner that reflects Christ?

_____

_____

_____

Conforming to the image of Christ is a gradual lifetime process, not an all-at-once experience. As we cultivate a relationship with the Potter and His transforming ways, we reflect more and more of His image. Often we're not aware of the personal changes until someone points them out to us. During these moments we can gratefully acknowledge the source of our transformation and rejoice in the increasing freedom of saying no to sin and yes to God. He has influenced our desires.

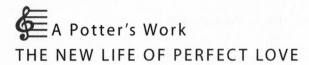

A Potter's Work
THE NEW LIFE OF PERFECT LOVE

The Chinese philosopher Lao Tzu reminds us that even a journey of a thousand miles must begin with a single step. What, then, is the first step on the Christian transformational journey? Christians have applied a variety of words to this first step—conversion, purgation, repentance, to name a few. Jesus also referred to the first step with a variety of terms. Sometimes, he encouraged people to repent of their sins. Other times he asked them to follow him. And sometimes he simply asks them to allow him to heal them. All seemed invited the same response—death to their old kingdom of self and an awakening of a new life of surrender to Perfect Love.

Stepping onto the road of Christian spiritual transformation requires an encounter with the living God. This encounter may be gradual or it may be sudden. But it will always involve a turning and an awakening.… Christian conversion is the most radical change process in human history. So much more than a mere change of the externals of our life, it is the refashioning of our entire being. The scope of transformation it entails makes even the most extravagant claims of therapeutic psychology pale by comparison.[2]
—*David Benner,* Surrender to Love

About Your Life

1. What radical changes have you experienced since accepting Jesus Christ as Savior?

_____

_____

_____

2. How is your life being refashioned to become like Jesus?

_____

_____

_____

3. What is your role in this process of spiritual transformation? What is God's role?

_____

_____

_____

Exploring Your Clay
THE NATURE OF YOUR DESIRES

Our desires affect how we live. We pursue what we crave. Romans 8:5–6 (NIV) explains, "Those who live according to the sinful nature have their minds set on what that nature desires; but those who live in accordance with the Spirit have their minds set on what the Spirit desires. The mind of sinful man is death, but the mind controlled by the Spirit is life and peace."

Conforming to Christ means transforming our desires. Again, this isn't an unwelcome effort on our part. Rather, it's a natural, trusting outflow of a love for the Potter.

Read the excerpt on page 180 and answer the accompanying questions. Then use the following questions to consider the nature of your desires—what they are now and what you want them to be.

1. How would you describe your current desire to be like Jesus?

_____

_____

_____

2. What natural desires get in the way of your becoming like Christ?

_____

_____

_____

3. At what time in your life have you desired Jesus the most? What were the circumstances? How did this desire unleash into your life?

_____

_____

_____

4. What is your top-of-the-box image for becoming like Christ?

_____

_____

_____

5. What do you really want to do with your life? How does conforming to Christ's image affect that desire?

_____

_____

_____

It's crucial to note that when we walk in the Spirit, our desires and God's desires can coincide. Some people erroneously think if they really desire something, it must not be God's will. But when we conform to Christ's image, he wants to fulfill our heart's desires. Psalm 37:3–4 (NIV) claims, "Trust in the LORD and do good.... Delight yourself in the LORD, and he will give you the desires of your heart." To cultivate Christlike desires, we concentrate on our spiritual walk, our intimacy with the Potter.

Soul Impressions
TAKING A SPIRITUAL AUDIT

How would you rate your spiritual life now? What do you want it to be? Turn to page 188 and use Worksheet 17—"A Spiritual Audit"—to assess the current state of your soul. The questions might clarify your desire for spiritual growth in the coming year. During the assessment, be careful not to feel like you're falling spiritually short; be inspired to transform your future.

In the next section, evaluate which spiritual disciplines could enhance that growth and mold your image to Christ's image.

On the Wheel
MAKING SPACE FOR GOD

The spiritual disciplines have been defined as "making space for God." They're tools for spending time with him and turning inward. Throughout the church's history, spiritual disciplines have helped believers grow to be more like Jesus. In fact, you've encountered several of these disciplines while using this workbook. For example, study, prayer, worship, solitude, confession, journaling, and contemplation are disciplines that contribute to our spiritual growth.

As you finish *Soul Shaping*, consider how you can continue using spiritual disciplines for your ongoing spiritual transformation. Worksheet 18—"Growing with the Disciplines"—on page 191 presents some of the spiritual disciplines. It will help you evaluate disciplines that could help you make room for God every day.

Prayers to the Potter
MAKING THE COMMITMENT

As a commitment to your spiritual transformation, pray or sing the words of this hymn, "Have Thine Own Way, Lord," to God the Potter.

Have Thine own way, Lord! Have Thine own way!

Thou art the potter, I am the clay.

Mold me and make me after Thy will,

While I am waiting, yielded and still.

Have Thine own way, Lord! Have Thine own way!

Hold o'er my being absolute sway.

Fill with Thy Spirit till all shall see

Christ only, always, living in me![3]

Notes for the Journey
ON FINDING QUIET TIME

Without solitude, it is virtually impossible to live a spiritual
life.... We do not take the spiritual life seriously if we do not
set aside time to be with God and listen to him.

—Henri Nouwen

Over the margins of life comes a whisper ... a faint call, a premonition of
richer living which we know we are passing by. Strained by the very mad pace
of our daily outer burdens, we are further strained by an inward uneasiness
because we have hints that there is a way of life vastly richer and deeper than
all this hurried existence, a life of unhurried serenity and peace and power.

—Thomas Kelly

In the silence, all our usual patterns assault us.... That is why most
people give up rather quickly. When Jesus was led by the Spirit into
the wilderness, the first things to show up were the wild beasts.

—Richard Rohr

Because we do not rest we lose our way.... Poisoned by the hypnotic belief
that good things come only through unceasing determination and tireless
effort, we never truly rest. And for want of rest, our lives are in danger.

—Wayne Muller

Let him who cannot be alone beware of community. Let him
who is not in community beware of being alone.

—Dietrich Bonhoeffer

Worksheet Seventeen
A SPIRITUAL AUDIT

Audit your life. An audit is a review and appraisal of a current condition. A spiritual audit can help you look at the state of your soul and desires now. Use these twelve questions to conduct your own audit. Then ask, "How do I feel about my spiritual life now?"

1. Am I content with who I am becoming? Why or why not?

_____

_____

_____

2. How has this past year shaped me?

_____

_____

_____

3. What has changed in me that I like?

_____

_____

_____

4. What do I think God is pleased with in my life now?

_____

_____

_____

5. Am I becoming less religious and more like Jesus? Elaborate.

_____

_____

_____

6. Do my friends and family recognize my growing desire to become like Jesus Christ? If so, what indicators might they observe?

_____

_____

_____

7. What is the state of my soul right now? Explain.

_____

_____

_____

8. Am I carrying baggage that affects my relationship with God and others?

_____

_____

_____

9. What is my main reason for getting up every day?

_____

_____

_____

10. Is my passion to be like Jesus burning or waning? Describe it.

_____

_____

_____

11. What would Jesus have me become this next year?

_____

_____

_____

12. In the next thirty days, what can I do to be more like Christ?

_____

_____

_____

Worksheet Eighteen
GROWING WITH THE DISCIPLINES

Making room for God. The spiritual disciplines can enhance your change process. As you draw closer to God, you can listen more clearly to Him and your own soul. Begin this worksheet by reading the two excerpts from Dallas Willard's *Divine Conspiracy* and Jan Johnson's excellent series of study guides on the spiritual disciplines, *Spiritual Disciplines Bible Study Guides*. Then read about specific disciplines that enhance spiritual transformation, considering how they could assist you.

A spiritual discipline is an activity within our power that we repeatedly and regularly engage in to enable us to do what we cannot do without engaging in the discipline. Spiritual disciplines are designed to help us become active and effective in the spiritual realm or our own heart, now spiritually alive by grace, in relation to God and His kingdom. They are designed to help us shift our dependence from human or natural to the ultimate reality, which is God and His kingdom. God works through the disciplines to help us experience a heightened intimacy with Him.

Dallas Willard shares, "For example, I fast from food to know that there is another food that sustains me. I memorize and meditate on Scripture so that the order of God's kingdom would become the order and power of my mind and life. Somewhat ironically, perhaps, all of the 'spiritual' disciplines are, or essentially involve, bodily behaviors...."[4]

Jan Johnson writes, "Have you ever wondered how God changes people? Maybe it seems as if old habits never change—no matter how hard you try. Maybe you've become discouraged with your lack of growth into Christlikeness. You know that you are forgiven through Jesus' suffering on the cross, and you realize that you are totally accepted by God on that basis. This is wonderful. And yet your desire to live in a way that pleases God somehow constantly falls short of the mark.

"God desires to transform our souls. This transformation occurs as we recognize that God created us to live in an interactive relationship with the Trinity. Our task is not to transform ourselves, but to stay connected with God in as much of life as possible. Our task is to do the connecting while God does the perfecting.

"As we connect with God, we gradually begin acting more like Christ. We become more likely to weep over our enemies instead of discrediting them. We're more likely to give up power instead of taking control. We're more likely to point out another's successes rather than grab the credit. Connecting with God changes us on the inside and we slowly become the tenderhearted, conscientious people our families always wished we'd become. This transformation of our souls through the work of the Holy Spirit results in 'Christ in you, the hope of glory (Col. 1:27).' We connect with God through spiritual disciplines or exercises."[5]

Thinking about the disciplines. What are some of the benefits of practicing spiritual disciplines or spiritual exercises? Think about these reasons.

1. **We practice our faith the way Jesus practiced His faith. We simply do what Jesus did. When Jesus said He is the way to God in John 14:6, He also showed us the way to live. Jesus practiced solitude. So can we. Jesus prayed. So can we.**

2. **Spiritual disciplines help us train in the right way. Like physical exercise, spiritual exercises build up what needs to be developed internally. The "Christ in you" emerges as we engage in spiritual exercises that honor Him.**

3. **Spiritual disciplines have proven their worth through the ages. These ancient exercises have stood the ravages of time, nourishing believers since the beginning of Christianity.**

4. **Spiritual disciplines help us cooperate with God to form us into mature, vibrant Christians. These are some of the ways we can "work out our salvation" that Paul mentions in Philippians 2:12–13.**

There are many spiritual disciplines, but the ones highlighted below and on the next page are good practice to begin your journey of spiritual transformation. For more information, see the "For Further Study" list at the end of this workbook. Consider how they can assist your spiritual transformation.

1. **Celebration: becoming spiritually alive in God and other people's presence. It's worship and proclaiming God's worth. We affirm what is true about Jesus, each other, and ourselves. We build up and encourage one another through music, singing, Scripture reading, and prayers of thanksgiving. Celebration is also taking the time to affirm, validate, and recall the belovedness of each other. It is the practice of "rejoicing with those who rejoice."**

2. **Contemplation: learning to become reflective and not just reactive. By taking time to reflect and consider, we learn to hear the Holy Spirit's voice. It's the art of**

becoming curious. We explore what lies underneath the surface and dive deep for truth.

3. Fellowship: joining others on the journey toward spiritual transformation. Creating safe places for genuine heart-to-heart sharing. It is "practicing the presence of people" and creating companionship.

4. Guidance: seeking guidance is different from getting advice or being taught. Guidance affirms us when we feel lost or confused. It helps us pursue God and Christlike living. However, we're also open to someone gently challenging us.

5. Journaling: many of the biblical psalms are David's journals. He poured out his heart to God with honest and confessional written words. We can do the same.

6. Submission: an awkward exercise for many people. Yielding to others on the journey helps empty ourselves of arrogance, pride, and the lone-ranger mentality. We learn to value wisdom, maturity, and people further along on the journey than we are.

7. Prayer: a conversation with God. It can be spoken, recited, wordless, or written. Prayer can be decisive, bewildered, submissive, or questioning.

8. Silence: Henri Nouwen calls silence "the furnace of transformation." We intentionally grow quiet to listen to God's voice.

9. Solitude: learning to be alone with God. As we practice solitude, we shut out other voices so we can hear God's words.

10. Study and Reading: In *Shadowlands*, Anthony Hopkins portraying C. S. Lewis says, "We read to know we are not alone." Many voices can speak to our journey, past and present. We grow better informed about the path ahead and how others navigated their journeys.

1. After reviewing the list, circle the disciplines that could enhance your spiritual transformation process. Why would these circled disciplines be helpful? List them and explain.

_____

_____

_____

2. Which of these disciplines do you already practice? How are they working for you?

_____

_____

_____

3. Do you need to improve upon, increase the frequency of, or drop any of the disciplines that you've tried to date? If so, which ones and how?

_____

_____

_____

4. How can you learn more about the disciplines you'd like to add?

_____

_____

_____

5. How can you begin using these new disciplines?

_____

_____

_____

FOR FURTHER STUDY

The following resources can enhance your spiritual transformation. Use this list as a springboard for exploring spiritual formation and transformation.

SESSION ONE: Soul Journey

Howard Baker, *Soul Keeping* (Colorado Springs, CO: NavPress, 1998).
   A wonderful introduction to spiritual direction and soul care.

Alister McGrath, *The Journey: A Pilgrim in the Lands of the Spirit* (New York: Galilee, 1999).
   A work rich with meaning and thought about journey themes and how to navigate the soul's path.

Robert Mulholland, *Invitation to a Journey: A Road Map for Spiritual Formation* (Downers Grove, IL: InterVarsity Press, 1993).
   A wonderful expression of what it means to become like Christ. It explores the process of spiritual formation.

SESSION TWO: You Are the Beloved

David Benner, *The Gift of Being Yourself* (Downers Grove, IL: InterVarsity Press), 2004.
   An important work that assists self-exploration and acceptance.

Henri Nouwen, *Life of the Beloved* (New York: Crossroad Publishing, 1995).
   One of the most crucial books written about our belovedness to God.

Henri Nouwen, *The Return of the Prodigal Son* (New York: Doubleday, 1992).
   A spiritual classic. A book to help reclaim much of what might have been lost on our spiritual journey.

Brennan Manning, *Abba's Child* (Colorado Springs: NavPress, 1994).
   A heartfelt invitation to explore the theme of belonging to God.

SESSION THREE: Trusting the Potter's Hands

Larry Crabb, *Shattered Dreams* (Colorado Springs: WaterBrook Press, 2001).
   An insightful book for navigating between pain and joy.

Philip Yancey, *Disappointment with God* (Grand Rapids: Zondervan, 1988).
   An honest journey into our doubts about God.

SESSION FOUR: Your Fearful and Wonderful Form

Parker Palmer, *Let Your Life Speak* (San Francisco: Jossey-Bass Publishing, 2000).
   Simply a must-read for every person on the journey. Palmer's treatment on vocation and listening to the voice within is one of the best treatments on the subject I know. Also, the chapter on depression is worth the price of the book.

Michael Yaconelli, *Messy Spirituality* (Grand Rapids: Zondervan Publishing House, 2002).
   An honest and straightforward look at the spiritual life, with its ups and downs.

SESSION FIVE: The Need to Reform

Brennan Manning, *Ruthless Trust* (San Francisco: HarperCollins, 2000).
   Explores both our ability and inability to trust God working in our lives.

Larry Crabb, *The Safest Place on Earth* (Nashville: Word Publishers, 1999).
   Explores how community helps us do soul work.

John Ortberg, *The Life You've Always Wanted* (Grand Rapids: Zondervan, 1997).
   Ortberg's treatment is often called, "Dallas (Willard) for Dummies." A readable and enjoyable book.

SESSION SIX: The Heart of Transformation

Bruce Demarest, *Soul Guide: Following Jesus as Spiritual Director* (Colorado Springs: NavPress, 2003).
   A wonderful exploration of Christ's ways of guiding people from their souls.

Stephen Smith, "The Transformation of a Man's Heart." Chapter One
   of *The Transformation of a Man's Heart* (Downers Grove, IL: InterVarsity Press, 2005).
   Explores authentic transformation and pseudotransformation, and how a person changes. Written for men, but applicable to women as well.

Stephen Smith, *Embracing Soul Care: Making Space for What Matters Most* (Grand Rapids: Kregel, 2006).
   Brief devotionals on transforming and taking care of the soul.

SESSION SEVEN: The Potter's Tools

Fil Anderson, *Running on Empty* (Colorado Springs: WaterBrook Press, 2004).
   Fil offers us an honest look at developing a more contemplative heart in the midst of harried times.

Keith R. Anderson, and Randy D. Reese, *Spiritual Mentoring* (Downers Grove, IL: InterVarsity Press, 1999).
   One of the best resources on spiritual mentoring and offering spiritual direction. A great overview.

Ruth Haley Barton, *Invitation to Solitude and Silence* (Downers Grove, IL: InterVarsity Press, 2004).
   If I were to buy one book on the spiritual disciplines, it would be this one to start with and grow
   from your experience with this book.

Ken Gire, *The Reflective Life* (Colorado Springs: Cook Communications, 1998).
   A wonderful place to begin to learn what it means to become more reflective in life.

Wayne Oates, *Nurturing Silence in a Noisy Heart: How to Find Inner Peace* (Minneapolis: Augsburg
   Publishing, 1996).
   A well-written guide on how to do just what the book implies in the title

Dallas Willard, *The Spirit of the Disciplines: Understanding How God Changes Lives* (San Francisco:
   HarperCollins, 1988). Richard Foster called this book when it was published, "The book of the
   decade." I agree even now.

SESSION EIGHT: The Freedom to Conform

David Benner, *Surrender to Love* (Downers Grove: InterVarsity Press, 2003).
   A touching book about God's love.

Adele Calhoun, *Spiritual Disciplines Handbook* (Downers Grove, IL: InterVarsity Press, 2005).
   A wonderful overview of many spiritual disciplines with suggestions for practicing them.

Jan Johnson, *Spiritual Discipline Bible Study Guides* (Downers Grove, IL: InterVarsity Press, 2003).
   These eight guides on some of the most frequently used spiritual disciplines offers excellent insight
   and study into this subject.

Henri Nouwen, *The Way of the Heart* (New York: Ballantine, 1981).
   Insights into solitude and silence, and living as Jesus and the early church fathers did.

John Piper, *Desiring God* (Sisters, OR: Multnomah Press, 1986).
   Piper's treatment on becoming a Christian hedonist is a must-read to challenge our long held
   beliefs about God.

Dallas Willard, *Hearing God* (Downers Grove, IL: InterVarsity Press, 1999).
   Explores a conversational relationship with God.

ABOUT THE POTTER'S INN

Potter's Inn is a Christian ministry founded by Stephen W. and Gwen Harding Smith, and is dedicated to the work of spiritual formation. A resource to the local church, organizations, and individuals, Potter's Inn promotes the themes of spiritual transformation to Christians on the journey of spiritual formation by offering

- guided retreats
- soul care
- books, small group guides, works of art, and other resources that
- explore spiritual transformation

Steve and Gwen travel throughout the United States and the world offering spiritual direction, soul care, and ministry to people who long for deeper intimacy with God. Steve is the author of *Soul Custody, The Lazarus Life: Spiritual Transformation for Ordinary People, Living the Lazarus Life, Embracing Soul Care: Making Space for What Matters Most,* and *Soul Shaping: A Practical Guide for Spiritual Transformation.*

is a thirty-five acre ranch and retreat nestled in the Colorado Rockies near Colorado Springs, Colorado. As a small, intimate retreat, Potter's Inn at Aspen Ridge is available for individual and small group retreats. "Soul Care Intensives"—guided retreats with spiritual direction—are available for leaders in the ministry and the marketplace. For more information or for a closer look at our artwork and literature, visit our website, www.pottersinn.com.

Or contact us at:

Potter's Inn
4050 Lee Vance View
Colorado Springs, CO 80918
Telephone: 719-264-8837

Email: resources@pottersinn.com

Potter's Inn Resources

Books

Soul Shaping: A Practical Guide for Spiritual Transformation by Stephen W. Smith (David C Cook, 2011). Steve uses the timeless image of the potter and clay to help us understand our shaping process. Key themes are Being the Beloved, Being Formed, Being Reformed, Being Transformed, and Being Conformed to the Image of Jesus Christ. Ideal for those wanting to know more about spiritual formation and how God shapes us throughout our lives.

Soul Custody: Choosing to Care for the One and Only You by Stephen W. Smith (David C Cook, 2010). Steve describes the state of violence and busyness that is affecting our souls. He offers eight choices to help us care for our souls. This book is for men and women and has study questions at the end of each chapter, making it ideal for small-group and class use.

The Lazarus Life by Stephen W. Smith (David C Cook, 2008). Lazarus the friend of Jesus frames the story of this unique book. His illness, death, and eventual resurrection mirror the story of transformation and how a person really changes. The graveclothes become a metaphor for us to explore the issues of our past and present that prevent us from changing and growing.

Living the Lazarus Life by Stephen W. Smith (David C Cook, 2009). This is the guidebook for *The Lazarus Life*. It is an ideal companion for individual, group, and class use. Divided into weekly sessions, this guidebook is designed to explore the themes of the book with probing questions, exercises, and creative Bible studies.

The Transformation of a Man's Heart compiled and edited by Stephen W. Smith (IVP, 2006). Steve asked various men to write chapters on the key themes of a man's heart where transformation is needed most in life. A man's past, vocation, marriage, sex, friendship, legacy, and relationship with God are covered. Ideal for men but also helpful for the women who love them. **The Transformation of a Man's**

Heart series has four separate study guides: **Transformation, Work, Marriage,** and **Sex**. The study guides are perfect for men's groups to discuss the key issues where men struggle and need to experience transformation. Contributors include: Howard Baker, Gordon Dalbey, Gary Chapman, James Houston, D. Ross Campbell, and others.

Embracing Soul Care by Stephen W. Smith (Kregel, 2006). In this book, you'll find short devotional readings about caring for the soul. Ideal for quiet times and for couples or families to read together. Also great for group use. The end of each reading features three questions to help you probe into your own soul and reflect on the topic.

Gifts

The Beloved Ring: A sterling silver and individually made ring for men and women. This beautiful ring is the perfect gift to yourself or someone you want to remind of his or her true identity as The Beloved. The word *Beloved* is engraved twice on the ring.

The Forming Hands Pendant: This pendant is 5/8" in height and is made of sterling silver showing the two distinct hands of the Potter—one hand being strong, the other being tender. Worn as a necklace or on a bracelet.

Available at www.pottersinn.com or in bookstores throughout the world. Please inquire about multiple copies for groups, classes, and churches for higher discounts.

Potter's Inn
4050 Lee Vance View
Colorado Springs, CO 80918
Telephone: 719.264.8837
Email: resources@pottersinn.com

About the Author

Stephen Smith, the primary writer and general editor of Potter's Inn products, is a gifted communicator to the everyday Christian. He is the spiritual director of Potter's Inn ministry, which he cofounded with his wife, Gwen.

Steve and Gwen have been involved in ministry since 1979. They've planted and led churches in North America and Europe. Steve has spoken to churches in North America, Europe, Africa, and Haiti. He frequently addresses student groups on college campuses through InterVarsity, Campus Crusade, and Athletes in Action. He is also a former adjunct professor of preaching at Tyndale Theological Seminary in Badhovedorph, the Netherlands, and is currently an adjunct teacher at Missionary Training International in Monument, Colorado. The Smiths travel internationally working with leaders and workers all over the world.

While living in Europe in the 1980s, Steve ministered behind the Iron Curtain in churches in Poland, the former East Germany, and Romania. In Poland and Romania he helped to foster partnerships with churches smuggling Bibles and food to Christians. He studied at Lenoir Rhyne College, Southern Baptist Theological Seminary, and Trinity Evangelical Divinity School. He was born in Charlotte, North Carolina.

Gwen, a registered nurse, was born and raised in Ethiopia as a "third-culture kid." She studied at Covenant College and University of North Carolina at Charlotte, where she received a bachelor's degree. She also studied at Denver Seminary in Denver, Colorado, and the Reformed Seminary in Orlando, Florida. Gwen served as a missionary nurse in West Africa and currently leads women's studies and retreats. She serves as a spiritual director for Potter's Inn ministry. Gwen and Steve have four sons and four daughters-in-law. The couple enjoys being in the outdoors, taking in God's glory in nature, reading, writing, and a strong cup of coffee.

NOTES

NOTES

NOTES

Endnotes

INTRODUCTION

1. Dallas Willard quoted in Bruce Demarest, *Soul Guide* (Colorado Springs: NavPress, 2003), 49.
2. Janet O. Hagberg and Robert A. Guelich, *The Critical Journey: Stages in the Life of Faith* (Salem, WI: Sheffield, 1989), 5.

SESSION ONE

1. *Webster's New World Dictionary* (Nashville: Southwestern, 1964), 158.
2. Robert M. Hamma, *Landscapes of the Soul: A Spirituality of Place* (Notre Dame, IN: Ave Maria Press, 1999), 41.

SESSION TWO

1. Eugene Peterson, *The Message* (Colorado Springs: NavPress, 2002), 222.
2. As quoted at www.oakleafpottery.com by Roy Yoder, November 2, 2004.
3. Henri Nouwen, *Here and Now* (New York: Crossroad, 1997), 134.
4. Henri Nouwen, *Life of the Beloved* (New York: Crossroad, 2002), 95.
5. As quoted at www.oakleafpottery.com by Roy Yoder, November 2, 2004.
6. Adapted from "Soulful Indulgence" in *Embracing Soul Care* by Stephen W. Smith (Grand Rapids: Kregel, 2006), 57–58.

SESSION THREE

1. Charlotte F. Speight and John Toki, *Hands in Clay* (New York: McGraw-Hill, 2004), 199.
2. Search online for "The Return of the Prodigal by Rembrandt" to study the artist's depiction of the two hands of the father.
3. Macrina Wiederkehr, *Seasons of Your Heart* (San Francisco: HarperOne, 1991), 70–71.

SESSION FOUR

1. Judith Couchman, *Designing a Woman's Life* (Sisters, OR: Multnomah, 1995), 13.

SESSION FIVE

1. Steve Mattison, *The Complete Potter* (Hauppauge, NY: Barron's, 2003), 14.
2. William Shannon, *Silence on Fire* (New York: Crossroad, 2000), 6–7.
3. Eugene Peterson, *Leap Over a Wall* (New York: HarperOne, 1998), 54.

SESSION SIX

1. Jacqui Atkin, *Handbuilt Pottery Techniques Revealed* (Hauppauge, NY: Barron's, 2004), 14.
2. Debra Evans, *Women of Character* (Grand Rapids, MI: Zondervan, 1995), n.p.
3. Robert Mulholland, *Invitation to a Journey* (Downers Grove, IL: InterVarsity, 1993), 25.
4. Paul Tournier, *A Listening Ear* (London: Hodder and Stoughton, 1987).
5. Used by permission from InterVarsity Press. First appeared in *The Transformation of a Man's Heart*, edited by Stephen W. Smith (Downers Grove, IL: InterVarsity Press, 2006).

SESSION SEVEN

1. John Dickerson, *Pottery Making: A Complete Guide* (New York: Viking, 1974), 9.

SESSION EIGHT

1. Alex McErlain, *Art of Throwing* (Ramsbury, Marlborough, Wiltshire, England: Crowood, 2002), 39.
2. David Benner, *Surrender to Love* (Downers Grove, IL: InterVarsity Press, 2003), 73–74.
3. "Have Thine Own Way, Lord" written in 1907 by Adelaide A. Pollard (lyrics) and George C. Stebbins (music). Public domain.
4. Dallas Willard, *The Divine Conspiracy* (New York: HarperOne, 1998), 353.
5. Jan Johnson, *Solitude and Silence* from the *Spiritual Disciplines Bible Study Guides* (Downers Grove, IL: InterVarsity, 2003) 5–6.